Stories of

I0160979

Providential Deliverance

"*As in the Ancient Days*"

Compiled by

W. A. SPICER

A PRAYER for the latter days: "Awake, awake, put on strength, O arm of the Lord; awake, as in the ancient days." Isa. 51:9.

TEACH Services, Inc.
P U B L I S H I N G
www.TEACHServices.com • (800) 367-1844

Facsimile Reproduction

As this book played a formative role in the development of Christian thought and the publisher feels that this book, with its candor and depth, still holds significance for the church today. Therefore the publisher has chosen to reproduce this historical classic from an original copy. Frequent variations in the quality of the print are unavoidable due to the condition of the original. Thus the print may look darker or lighter or appear to be missing detail, more in some places than in others.

Copyright © 2023 TEACH Services, Inc.
ISBN-13: 978-1-5725-8102-9 (Paperback)
Library of Congress Control Number: 9660017

Published by

TEACH Services, Inc.
P U B L I S H I N G
www.TEACHServices.com • (800) 367-1844

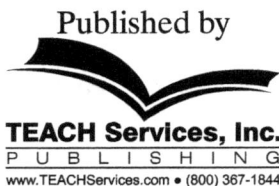

CONTENTS

FROM A PROCLAMATION

By Darius, King of Babylon, About 537 B. C.

"HE is the living God, and steadfast forever, and His kingdom that which shall not be destroyed, and His dominion shall be even unto the end. He delivereth and rescueth, and He worketh signs and wonders in heaven and in earth, who hath delivered Daniel from the power of the lions." Dan. 6:26, 27.

"AS IN THE ANCIENT DAYS"

"Awake, . . . O arm of the Lord; awake as in the ancient days." Isa. 51:9.

A Prayer for the Last Days

IT is plainly a prayer set for the children of God in the last days, that the prophet Isaiah records:

"Awake, awake, put on strength, O arm of the Lord; awake, as in the ancient days, in the generations of old. Art thou not it that hath cut Rahab [Egypt], and wounded the dragon? Art thou not it which hath dried the sea, the waters of the great deep; that hath made the depths of the sea a way for the ransomed to pass over?" Isa. 51:9, 10.

It is with trust in the living God who did things on earth in ancient Bible times, that the children of God in the last generation are to "come with singing unto Zion." The Lord reminds them that He is the same living God as in days of old: "I am the Lord thy God, that divideth the sea, whose waves roared: The Lord of Hosts is His name." Verse 15.

The stories of providential interventions and deliverances in the narratives of Holy Scripture are lessons for us today. As the book "Education" so aptly says:

"These things were not written merely that we might read and wonder, but that the same faith which wrought in God's servants of old might work in us. In no less marked a manner than He wrought then will He work now wherever there are hearts of faith to be channels of His power."
—*Page 256.*

Reviewing the providences of the ancient days, we sing with new fervor the old hymn:

> "Is not Thy grace as mighty now
> As when Elijah felt its power?
> When glory beamed from Moses' brow,
> Or Job endured the trying hour?

"Remember, Lord, the ancient days;
Renew Thy work, Thy grace restore;
And while to Thee our hearts we raise,
On us Thy Holy Spirit pour."
                                —*Bathurst.*

Fetters Loosed, Prison Doors Opened

The apostle Peter was in prison, held by Herod, condemned to death. He was chained to two Roman soldiers. It was in the dead of night. All were asleep. An angel touched Peter and woke him up. "His chains fell off from his hands," and the iron gate of the prison "opened to them of his own accord." (See Acts 12:5-11.) Peter was free in the street outside. "Now I know of a surety," said he to himself, "that the Lord hath sent His angel, and hath delivered me."

In times after the Reformation in Germany, a group of believers called "Brethren" were in prison in Moravia. David Nitschmann says that one evening he was impressed that he would escape that night. In a book, "Suppressed Evidence," Thomas Boys quotes Nitschmann's own story:

"I told my brethren that I had thoughts of leaving them that night. 'And I too,' instantly added David Schneider; 'I mean to go with you.' We had to wait till eleven. Not knowing how I should be able to get rid of my irons, I laid hands upon the padlock which fastened them, to try to open it with a knife; and behold, it was opened!

"I began to weep for joy, and I said to Schneider, 'Now I see it is the will of God that we should go.' "

They went out into the court to look for a ladder to scale the wall. But they found the first door open. And the outer door was open! "This was a second sign to us," he says. Out they went with joy, and hung their chains on the prison wall, thus leaving behind them a fine memorial of deliverance. They reached Herrnhut, in Saxony, where Count Zinzendorf was welcoming the refugees of conscience and preparing to organize them into the wonderful Moravian movement that led the way in modern missions. This same David Nitschmann was the pioneer in West Indian missions to the slaves on the plantations, ready, he said, to sell himself into slavery if necessary in order to give the gospel to those people.

In another prison, in those times, two Brethren realized that possibly the same angel that opened Peter's prison door was at work for them. Andrew Beyer had been kept in prison for more than a year, and tortured. Now his persecutors fixed the day when he was to be put into a damp, dark dungeon.

"The day on which his sentence was to be executed," says Bost's history of the Moravians, "David Fritsch, who was in the same prison, happened to push against the door. The great chain which was stretched across the outside gave way. They opened the door and fled." They took their families and escaped to Herrnhut, Count Zinzendorf's refuge—the place, by the way, where the Sabbath truth was discussed and to some extent followed, Zinzendorf himself regarding that day as the true day of rest.

What Frightened the Chinese Servant

At an annual meeting of the Shanghai Sanitarium, on Rubicon Road, Chaplain A. Mountain told us the story of a heathen Chinese servant who was stricken with fear as prayer was offered for her Christian mistress. Abbreviated, it is as follows:

The Chinese mistress was a Christian. Following a major operation, her life was in the balance. The sanitarium staff leaders met to offer special prayer for the lady. The servant was in the room. Immediately after prayer the patient revived and made a strong recovery. But it was noticed that the heathen servant had been frightened in the prayer service. She appeared to be afraid to stay in the room. Later, at their home, the servant was one day looking at the pictures in one of our Chinese books which her mistress was earnestly studying. In the book was a picture of an angel with wings outspread. "Oh!" cried the non-Christian servant, "that is a picture of what I saw when they prayed for you at the

Rubicon Road. One just like this came to your bedside and laid his hand on you there."

The Praying Church Surprised

While Peter was held in prison, awaiting death, "prayer was made without ceasing of the church unto God for him." Acts 12:5. After deliverance from the prison, Peter came to the house of Mary, the mother of John Mark, "where many were gathered together praying"—for his deliverance, of course. The servant maid at the door of the gate knew Peter's voice. Without waiting to open the gate, in her joy she ran in and told the praying group, "Peter is at the gate!" They said, "Thou art mad." "But Peter continued knocking: and when they had opened the door, and saw him, they were astonished." Verses 12-16. It was more than they could think possible.

In our own mission work in South America, a praying church was astonished at the answer to their prayers. Evangelist F. G. Lane told us of a youth named Miguel, who was arrested on the suspicion that he had stolen from his employer. The employer stood by him; but the police held him, trying by rigorous and painful means to extort a confession. The fetters were drawn so tight that his wrists were cut. Members of the mission interceded, urging that there was no evidence of guilt. "But the law requires us to hold a suspect two weeks," the officers said. As Friday night came, and the weekly prayer service, the church prayed earnestly for Miguel. After the meeting they talked; and then they had another season of prayer, continuing till near midnight.

Next morning the believers gathered for the Sabbath services. They met in the rear of the mission home, as it was an intensely Catholic city. A girl was left at the gate, to direct any stranger to the meeting room, which was reached by a side passage. Then, like the maid at the gate in Peter's day, this girl had a surprise. She saw a young man whom she knew, approaching the gate!

"Suddenly," says Evangelist Lane, "she came running back into the meeting room, crying, 'Miguel is coming! Miguel is coming!'

" 'No,' the people said; 'you must be mistaken. It cannot be Miguel.'

"But all hastily went out to see, and there was Miguel at the gate, smiling and joyful.

" 'How came it that you were released?' we asked.

" 'Well, I don't know,' he replied; 'only that the officers came and took off the chains, and told me I was free and could go.' "

So once again, as in the book of Acts, while the church prayed, the Lord surprised them by sending quick deliverance.

Infirmities Left at Water's Edge

Obeying the word of the Lord by Elisha the prophet, Naaman, the pagan Syrian captain, immersed himself seven times in the Jordan and found his leprosy washed away. "His flesh came again like unto the flesh of a little child." (See 2 Kings 5:1-14.) To a blind man in Jerusalem Jesus said, "Go, wash in the pool of Siloam;" and as the blind man rose from the pool, he "came seeing." John 9:7.

A Chinese man was reduced by blindness to poverty and begging. At a meeting, says Superintendent K. H. Wood, of our East China Union Mission, the blind man's heart laid hold of the gospel. Then,

"As the light of the advent message flooded his mind, the light of the sun penetrated his darkened eyes, and his sight was restored. He recognized this as a wonderful providence of God, and to him it was a token that this Sabbath and advent truth was the gospel message for this time. He gave himself to service, and three churches have been organized as a result of his work."

In Cuba a deaf man was baptized; and as he rose from the watery grave, he heard the singing of a hymn by the group standing at the water's edge. His hearing was restored as he obeyed the word of the Lord in baptism.

Supernaturally Stricken With Fear

The Syrian army had Samaria shut up. There was famine to the death in the city. The besiegers had only to hold on to win, humanly speaking. Then God intervened:

"The Lord had made the host of the Syrians to hear a noise of chariots, and a noise of horses, even the noise of a great host. . . . Wherefore they arose and fled in the twilight." 2 Kings 7:6, 7.

They left abundant stores of food for the hungry city.

Two Protestants, in Reformation times, were burned at the stake in Bordeaux, France. Though they were but two simple men, with no following, Foxe says that the magistrates had all gates locked and guarded as the fires were lighted. "And further," says Foxe, "to note the work of God that followed, when these two mild and martyred saints were almost consumed to ashes, suddenly, without cause, such a fear fell upon them that justices and people fled in such haste that they overran one another. The prior of St. Anthony's fell down, so that a great number went over him. The judge fled to a widow's house crying, 'Hide me, save my life!' Every man shut up his house. After the fear was past, every man asked what the matter was, but none could tell."

In our early days in Spain, Evangelist F. Bond was attacked in a house where he was preaching. A fanatical mob of people were smashing at doors and windows. "The only thing I could think of was to pray," the evangelist said. He lifted his voice in prayer, calling upon God above all the noise of the mob. "Within a few seconds," he said, "the mob fled. They had broken through the front door. They seemed determined to get in as if to tear us in pieces. But the moment I began to pray, they fled in terror. God surely must have spoken terror to the hearts of those people when we lifted up our hearts in prayer to the living God."

"Passing Through the Midst of Them"

The mob at Nazareth rose up and took Jesus to the brow of the hill, "that they might cast Him down headlong. But He passing through the midst of them went His way." Luke 4:30.

Their fury was restrained, their arms were made powerless to lay hold of Him; perhaps their eyes were withheld from seeing.

During a meeting in Asia Minor, in prewar times, our pioneer worker, Evangelist Baharian, was beset by an Armenian Catholic mob that surrounded his meeting place. The believers had barricaded the door, but the attackers were digging through the wall. Stones smashed windows. "Kill the heretic!" was the cry. As the wall was dug through, the brethren said: "Now is the time to go!" They opened the door. "We stepped out into the face of the crowd," the evangelist told us, "and passed through them. They were pulling and hauling one another to get at the preacher; but all the way not a particle of harm resulted." The party "passed through the midst of them," and reached the house of the mayor, who immediately provided horses and soldiers and sent the evangelist out of the village. Not a hand, he told us, was laid upon him, though, humanly speaking, he was in their power, and they thirsted for his life.

Guided to the Place to Begin

With much work still to do in Asia Minor, the apostle Paul sought to go into the province of Asia. But the Spirit forbade him. Then he and his helpers turned to go into Bithynia, "but the Spirit suffered them not." They came to Troas, seaport for ships to Europe, and there came the vision, "Come over into Macedonia, and help us." It was a call to open work in Europe; and at Philippi, among believing women who were praying for light, the apostle began. Acts 16.

In the early days of our work in Oregon, Evangelist Tabor was turned to the right place. He told me this experience:

"I was asked by the conference to go to C—— to open work. But as I prepared to go, the conviction kept coming, 'Go to A——.' At last I told the brethren, and they said, 'Go to A——.' On my way, the impression came vividly to my mind (how imparted I could not tell) of a certain street, on which, after following it several blocks, I should find the house in which to begin the work.

"Reaching A——, I found the street, and followed it; there was the house answering to the distinct impression given me. I called, and explained my mission as a Bible evangelist to the man of the house. 'The Lord must have sent you,' he said, 'for that is just what I wanted.' He opened his house for Bible study and cottage meetings, and as a result a church was raised up."

The Elements to the Rescue

When Sisera, captain of the host of Jabin, king of Canaan, led his mighty army against Israel in the days of Deborah and Barak, the very elements of the heaven were loosed against him: "They fought from heaven; the stars in their courses fought against Sisera." Judges 5:20. Perhaps it was like that time in Egypt when "the Lord sent thunder and hail, and the fire ran along upon the ground." Ex. 9:23.

In our early mission work among the Indians of the high Andes, fanatical superstition sometimes prompted plans to attack our stations. Generally these plans were remarkably frustrated. Speaking of these deliverances, Missionary E. F. Petersen wrote:

"At another time, as hostile Indians gathered for an attack upon one of our stations, a heavy storm came up, and down the road where the attackers must pass, the lightning seemed to flash almost continuously, running along the ground in long streaks, like fiery serpents, thus frightening them, and frustrating their evil purposes. It is wonderful how the Lord protects the work against all the efforts of the enemy to destroy it."

Earlier, in East Africa, the savage Akamba were marching by night on a mission house, with war cries and fire and spear. The mission family heard, and after having done what little they could to make doors and windows fast, fell to their knees in prayer. In her book, "In the Heart of Savagedom," Mrs. Stuart Watt tells how they were startled from their knees as deliverance was sent:

"We heard an unearthly detonating sound overhead, and springing to the door to see what was the matter, we found the heavens ablaze with light, and our eyes caught sight of a white-hot aerolite of immense proportions shooting across the firmament over our station. The gigantic fiery ball whizzed through the atmosphere with terrific velocity, illuminating the whole country with a lustrous, dazzling glow, and leaving behind it a great trail of fire as it disappeared, striking a mountain thirty miles distant.

"The huge meteorite had swept directly over the heads of the multitude of warriors, who were struck with such terror and mortal dread that they rushed panic-stricken to their homes among the hills."

Thereafter a great change was seen in the attitude of the people toward the mission. The victory had been won.

Judgment on Persecutors

Herod, king of the Jews, had slain James to please the Jews, and was still glorifying himself before the people. "Upon a set day" he made a great speech, and there and then "the angel of the Lord smote him." He perished suddenly in the midst of his plots and plans. "But the word of God grew and multiplied," the Scripture adds. Acts 12.

During the World War, when feeling ran high along the border countries, a certain Greek Orthodox Catholic priest set out to persecute the Adventists. He fell very ill, and was convicted that this had come upon him as a judgment. He vowed that he would no more persecute these believers if God would forgive and restore him. Immediately he was well. His wife told the story in the town. (The Greek priests marry, it should be remembered.) But later he resumed his persecutions, more bitterly than ever. Here is the sequel, as brethren told me the story when we traveled in that region just after the war:

"He searched out all the homes of the Adventists. He found their retired place of Sabbath meetings.

"He saw the police, and arranged that the next Sabbath

2

the place of meeting should be raided by armed soldiers, and all the Adventists taken. 'I will root them out of ——!' he declared.

"All was in readiness on Friday evening. The priest's plans were well laid. Next morning the group of Adventists were to be caught in the snare. He returned to his home, well content with the arrangement.

"As he sat in his chair at home, he related to his wife his plans; and then he asked her to bring in the evening tray, with food and drink.

"The wife went out to prepare the meal, and when she returned with the food, she found the priest sitting in his chair, dead.

"The wife had told the story of his former sickness, of his vow to cease persecuting, and of his recovery. Now that experience was recalled by the people, and the fear of God came upon the hearts of multitudes. 'It is not a good thing to persecute these people,' it was freely said."

The Parted Flame: How Africa Spoke to Asia

AN African deliverance kindled the light of faith far across in Asia. It shows that it is good to "declare His glory among the heathen, His wonders among all people." Ps. 96:3.

In the early days of missions in Rhodesia, when our first station in the Somabula district was under construction, Missionary F. B. Armitage told of a deliverance by the parting of the flames on one occasion when he was on a journey from home. He said:

"I started from the station early in the morning. Toward evening a little boy came running into the tent where Mrs. Armitage was at work, crying, "There is fire in the grass! There is fire in the grass!'

"Our mission was in a valley, and down the valley somewhere a fire had been started and was sweeping toward the station. The season had been dry, and the grass was like tinder, standing, in places, as high as a man's head. One can imagine how that fire would look to the mission family, with only the orphan children and Mrs. Armitage and her own little one on the premises. We had been at this place only a short time, and had not had time to make fireguards or take any other precautions. The situation was indeed desperate.

"For a few startled moments Mrs. Armitage watched the oncoming flames, and then to herself she said, 'Our heavenly Father has never failed us yet, and I believe He will not leave us now.'

"There might have been a chance for flight, but there was the mission station, with all that it represented of struggle and toil and future fruitfulness in the saving of souls. She turned to the text that had been the deciding word in our

17

entering Africa, and our stay and support in many a trying experience. Again she read the promise, 'Fear thou not; for I am with thee: be not dismayed; for I am thy God: I will strengthen thee; yea, I will help thee; yea, I will uphold thee with the right hand of My righteousness.' Isa. 41:10.

"The assurance came to her heart that she was not left alone, and she said, 'Our Father will take care of us once more, I am sure.'

"Still the fire came leaping on. It was of no use to think of trying to fight it, with only the little orphan children to help. It came to within seventy yards of the station, and there it went out in front, the flames dividing and passing by on each side of the farm, joining farther up the valley and sweeping on beyond. The mission was saved.

"That night I saw by the red glow that there was fire in the valley. Hurrying homeward with all speed, I found, to my deepest joy, not only my family and the children safe, but the mission preserved as well. All about the mission the grass was dry, but there stood a five-acre plot untouched. The fire had stopped right in the dry grass, and no one could say why, save as we understand that the promises of our heavenly Father are sure, and that He will not leave us nor forsake us when we trust Him and are in the way of duty."

The Answering Deliverance in China

This story of the parted flames on the African veld was told, years later, in Asia. Director A. L. Ham, of South China, preaching in the Cantonese language to a mixed audience of Christians and non-Christians, told how the prayer of faith in faraway Africa must have brought an angel from heaven to part the flames and save the mission home. One listener was a Chinese woman, not yet a Christian.

The story gripped her heart. How good to know a God who cares, a living God who has angels of deliverance at His command!

Some time later a furious fire broke out in the section of the town where this Chinese listener had her home and property. The wind was sweeping the flames down the narrow streets. The lightly built houses were as dry as tinder. The flames came roaring on, straight for the Chinese woman's home.

Now she thought of the story of that deliverance on the African plains, which the pastor had told to impress the lesson of faith. She needed the same help.

"O God of the Christians," she prayed, "help me and deliver me now!"

As she prayed this prayer of struggling faith, the deliverance came. The fire parted, and swept by on either side. Only her kitchen was scorched, as though the flame left a mark there of the peril from which God had saved her.

"And how did she come out after this?" I asked.

"She was convicted that the true God had heard her prayer," Director Ham replied. "She gave her heart to earnest study of the gospel, and later became a baptized member."

It is to help the steps of faith to find sure footing in the divine assurances of care, that the stories of supernatural intervention are recorded in Scripture. As one of the apostles wrote:

"Many other signs truly did Jesus in the presence of His disciples, which are not written in this book: but these are written, that ye might believe." John 20:30, 31.

Even so, it is good to put on record and keep in memory some of the signal tokens of the Intervening Hand in these modern times. God's hand is truly over all His works in our day, as in ancient Bible times; and as we see these tokens of His special watchcare in places of need or peril, we are helped to trust His tender care in all the unseen ways of the daily round of ordinary home life. The daily blessings of His love and grace and providence are over us continually.

> "Since from His bounty I receive
> Such proofs of love divine,
> Had I a thousand hearts to give,
> Lord, they should all be Thine."

Volcanic Fires Parted

In Java, in the East Indies, on the slopes of Mt. Kloet, lived an elderly Chinese woman, a member of our church. She was particularly happy in bringing in her tithe, her only income being from her garden on the edge of the village. Missionary Albert Munson reported her experience during the awful eruption of 1919, when Kloet spread devastation and death:

"Twice a year this Christian woman brings to the mission a bag of coppers—the tithe of her meager income.

"During the eruption of Kloet, it was thought that this aged Chinese believer must have been lost, and all hope for her safety was given up. Imagine the joyful surprise at the mission when one day, in she came as usual, with her bag of coppers!

"On being questioned as to her escape amid the disaster, she told how the burning lava poured down the slopes of the mountain, destroying villages and hundreds of lives. As the flood of fiery lava came to the top of her kampong, the lava stream suddenly divided, and passed on either side, leaving her village and its people unharmed, though they were in utter darkness for some time. As soon as she was able to travel through the debris and ruin left by the eruption over the mountainside, this aged Christian's first thought was to bring in her tithe, sacredly laid up for the work of God."

"AS IN THE GENERATIONS OF OLD"

"Whoso is wise, and will observe these things, even they shall understand the loving-kindness of the Lord." Ps. 107:43.

The Waves Were Calmed

IN peril on the stormy sea of Galilee the disciples awakened Jesus, saying, "Master, Master, we perish!" Their boat had filled with water. Then Jesus rebuked the storm, and "there was a calm." "Where is your faith?" He asked. The disciples were amazed, and said: "He commandeth even the winds and water, and they obey Him." Luke 8:24, 25. It is a lesson for every storm-tossed believer on the rough seas of life. The Master is ever by.

> "No water can swallow the ship where lies
> The Master of ocean, and earth, and skies."

From the South Seas comes a story of waves calmed at the cry of one of the Lord's missionary pioneers.

Our mission boat in the New Hebrides was on the high seas, J. D. Anderson, of Australia, in charge. A storm came up. The engine was running nicely and sails were folded. A voice seemed to say, "Put up your sails." But the missionary thought, "The engine is safer." Then came again that message, almost audible. "The engine will give out. Put up the sails!"

"Scarcely had the words been spoken," says Missionary Anderson, "when a small piece in the engine broke."

Now further instruction came. The missionary tells it:

"A voice seemed to say, 'You are going to turn over, but angels will lift the boat up, and you will speak, and the waves will be calm.' I said in prayer, 'O Lord, it is too much.' But again the voice spoke, 'Why be afraid? The angels will help you, and this will take place to show the boys that the God whom you serve is able to deliver.' I prayed the second time, saying, 'Thy will be done, O Lord, not mine.'

"We had not proceeded far when two large waves came. Charlie was holding the main sail and instructing two other boys who were holding the helm. The little boat was turned to meet the first wave all right, but was not able to right herself before the second wave caught her and seemed to stand her almost mast downward. All hands on deck were thrown into the sea. At the time, I was standing in the cabin with my head out, but was thrown headlong into the water. I cannot remember what happened to me then, but I do know that, although the worst swimmer of all, I was the first on deck. When I did re-collect myself, I was sitting on the side of the boat.

"As I sat there, the boat began in a miraculous way to right herself, notwithstanding the fact that everything was against her. Everything inside the boat was thrown to one side, and some of the boys were hanging on to the sunken side. One boy came up on the boom as the boat came up. As she righted, I remembered the words spoken to me regarding the waves,—'You will speak, and the waves will be calm,'—so I prayed and lifted up my hand to God, which was noticed by some of the boys; and for about fifty yards back from the boat the water appeared as smooth as a pool, nor did any waves of any size reach us again until we had everything righted and were well under sail.

"Charlie and I went into the cabin and thanked the Lord for the wonderful deliverance. The other five boys, who had never shown any interest in things of God, were astonished. On arriving at a safe anchorage, they could not talk quickly enough about it. They said, 'Truly your Chief is strong. If this had been any other boat, we would have all been drowned today.'"

Delivered as They Sang Praises

In the days of King Jehoshaphat, a great confederacy of enemies came against Judah. It seemed a hopeless case. "We have no might against this great company," Jehoshaphat prayed; "but our eyes are upon Thee." And "when they began to sing and to praise," we are told, the Lord sent confusion upon the hosts of Ammon and Moab and the forces of Mt. Seir, and they began to destroy one another. (See 2 Chronicles 20.)

In the days of the Moravian and Bohemian persecutions a company of the believers called "Brethren" found deliverance in song. It was in 1723. Bost, in his "History of the Bohemian and Moravian Brethren," repeats the story:

"On this occasion their enemies again came upon them with great force, for they feared the people. As they entered the place, the brethren began to sing, with a clear and strong voice, Luther's celebrated hymn:

> " 'If the whole world with devils swarmed,
> That threatened us to swallow,
> We will not fear, for we are armed,
> And victory must follow.
> We dare the devil's might,
> His malice, craft, and spite;
> Though he may us assail,
> He never shall prevail:
> The word of God shall conquer.'

"The officer demanded silence, when they repeated the verse a second, and third time, which struck him with such terror that he ran away, leaving behind him a number of books he had collected."

The Smitten Attackers

When the Assyrian army surrounded Jerusalem, and the leader sent to Hezekiah a boastful letter, telling what he would do to the Jews, King Hezekiah took that letter to the temple, "and spread it before the Lord." 2 Kings 19:14. Through the prophet Isaiah the Lord sent answer that the Assyrians would not so much as shoot an arrow into the city. "I will defend this city," said the Lord. "And it came to pass that night, that the angel of the Lord went out, and smote in the camp of the Assyrians a hundred fourscore and five thousand." Verse 35.

On my first visit to Africa, I met Mrs. Blaine, one of our

members, who told me how her grandfather, Mr. Tainton, one of the early missionaries to Africa, laid hold of this Bible story in his prayer for deliverance from savage warriors who had come down into Pondoland. He had a mission among the people of Faku, chief of the Pondos. Faku came to the missionary in distress. They had no strength to resist. "We shall be wiped off the earth," he wailed. Mrs. Blaine's account, as her grandmother used to tell it, runs thus:

" 'Faku,' said the missionary, 'do you remember what God did when you prayed for rain?'

" 'Yes,' said the chief.

" 'Well, come again with your people, and humble yourselves, and ask the Lord to save you out of the hands of the enemy. The Lord who saved His people from the hands of the Assyrians may be implored to save you now. What He did for Israel He can do for you, if it is to His glory.'

"So they came up to the mission; and they fasted and prayed for deliverance.

" ' They are now but two days' journey from our villages,' said Faku to the missionary, as messengers came in with the news.

" 'But you have prayed to God to save you,' said the missionary.

"After two days, Mr. Tainton said to Faku: 'Where are your enemies? Two days have passed, and we hear nothing of them.'

"So Faku sent out some men to search for the enemy. After several days' searching, they found their enemies, a large company of warriors, lying dead in their camp in a forest. Some disease, it was decided, had broken out suddenly among them, and they had perished together. But however it was, Faku thanked God that He had heard the cry of His people and sent deliverance."

The Spirits Beg for Terms

When Jesus was about to speak the word of healing to the two men, possessed, in the country of the Gergesenes, by the sea, the evil spirits within begged for terms: "They besought

Him that He would not command them to go out into the deep. And there was there a herd of many swine feeding on the mountain: and they besought Him that He would suffer them to enter into them. And He suffered them." Luke 8:31, 32.

In Korea a woman was possessed by evil spirits. The heathen people advised her husband to take her to the Christians. He brought her ten miles to a little church, where our Korean local elder and the believers prayed for her. The woman, who knew nothing of the Bible, was moved to fury against the Book at first, every time they read from it. After long prayer a change came. The evil spirits in the woman cried out that they were five. The late Missionary C. L. Butterfield, who visited the place, reported that those simple believers continued praying God that the spirits might be cast out.

"The spirits at last replied, 'Where will you send us?' The Korean leader answered, 'When Jesus was upon earth, He sent the evil spirits into the swine. You can go there.'

"But that was not what they wanted. They asked to be allowed to enter some other person, or to return to the same woman later. The Christians stoutly refused to consent, and continued to read the promises of the word of God, and to plead with Him that the evil spirits might be driven out.

"At last the spirits could resist no longer. 'We will leave in three days,' they said, speaking through the voice of the poor victim, 'and we will go to a certain small creek in the mountains.' Still the believers held on in prayer for the woman's deliverance. On the third day, with violent contortions, the woman was set free. Her mind became calm. The evil spirits had indeed left her. She gave her heart to God, and has since been faithful."

Soldiers Sent to the Rescue

The Jewish mob had seized Paul in the temple and were "about to kill him." But hearing the uproar, the Roman chief captain "immediately took soldiers and centurions, and ran down unto them." Acts 21:31, 32. Again, when Paul was allowed to speak before the council, and uproar followed, "the chief captain, fearing lest Paul should have been pulled in pieces of them, commanded the soldiers to go down, and take him by force from among them, and to bring him into the castle." Acts 23:10. The Roman soldiers, who had the apostle under surveillance and arrest, were his protectors.

During the World War, when feeling ran high, in one of the countries of Eastern Europe a bishop and his priests summoned all the Seventh-day Adventists in one city to appear in the central church. The incident was related at the Autumn Council of 1920 by L. H. Christian. The bishop denounced the Adventists, and called them to line up in front of the church. "Get down on your knees," he commanded. Simple peasant people, accustomed to obeying, they knelt—all except one woman, small of stature, but high of faith and courage. She remained standing. "Now, confess!" thundered the bishop. It looked as if they might do it. But the little woman was moved to stand up for truth:

"She ran to her husband, and seizing him by the shoulders, shouted, 'Is that man God? Are we going to pray to a bishop? Have we been taught the truth to no effect?' Then she said, 'In the name of the Lord, I command you, my brethren, every one to stand up.' They all got up and went back and took their seats.

"The bishop did not know what to do. The mob shouted that they would kill that little woman, and they were ready to tear her in pieces. Just then an officer came forward and said to the soldiers, 'Take your swords, and every one take a Seventh-day Adventist by the hand, and I will take that little woman.' All expected the Adventists to be killed, but they were surprised. Turning to the mayor, the officer said, 'You have a commission to protect the weak,' and to the bishop, 'You, bishop, were sent to preach the gospel.' Then he swung his sword and said, 'Clear the way and lead the Adventists home. If you ever molest the Seventh-day Adventists again, you will hear from me.'

"This meant much to that woman, and to the Adventists,

and to the cause of God in that city. The church there is of good cheer and very active."

Again and again soldiers sent to arrest our brethren or report upon our meetings have turned into guards to repress attacks by enemies.

Courage for Those Toiling Seemingly in Vain

One morning by the sea Jesus said to the disciples, "Launch out into the deep, and let down your nets." "Master," said Peter, "we have toiled all the night, and have taken nothing: nevertheless at Thy word I will let down the net." Luke 5:4, 5. And this time the net was broken by the catch.

Evangelist L. Gopal Mookerjee, of our East Bengal Mission, urged a fisherman to plan to attend a five-day general meeting. "But I am a poor man," he replied. "My wife has no proper clothes, and we seldom have two days' food ahead. If I ought to go, you will have to pray God to send me the money." And they did pray. That Bengali fisherman set his traps as usual that night. But it was not the usual catch that came. The traps were full. "I never had so much money before," he said, when he sold the catch. "He bought clothing for his wife, and together they went to the conference, where they gave their testimony to the delivering hand of God," wrote Evangelist Mookerjee, who added: "The Friend of the Galilean fishermen still lives."

A Chinese fisherman got into debt and was so discouraged that he stopped paying tithe and contemplated going out to work on the Sabbath. He had a son in the mission school. "Come," the boy said, "come to the meeting once more, and I will ask them to pray God to help you. Father, do come!" The father went to the Sabbath service. The church prayed; he confessed his wrong, and took his stand anew for Christ. And the Lord who encouraged the disciples when they had fished all night and "caught nothing," must surely have said again, even to this Chinese fisherman, "Cast the net on the right side of the ship" (John 21:3-6); for the mission report tells this sequel:

"That evening, starting out fishing, he was impressed to go in a direction opposite to that of his fellow fishermen. He himself was aware that it was not ordinarily a good place to fish, and also others told him not to go that way. But he heeded no one and went, following some inward guidance. It was not long before he had a load of fish worth a very large sum in Chinese wage.

"Some nights later, again going out in the evening, he had a draft of fishes yet larger, while all the rest of the men, who caught nothing, were greatly astonished. He paid all his debts, and bought for his boy, who is with us learning weaving, some new shoes and clothing. His joy as well as ours is great."

ALL the angels of heaven are sent forth to minister to the heirs of salvation. They are beyond numbering; and if so, then the earth is full of angels.

The accounts that come from every side, show that while most often they are seen only by those who need such witness, angel helpers are really abroad in the gospel work. The gospel worker or believer, who has the Bible, does not need to see them; he knows they are there. And the believers about the daily tasks at home or in business know that the unseen ministers are all about.

The Visitor in Court

In one of the Spanish-American countries where official sentiment was bitter against religious work, one of our evangelists was arrested and thrown roughly into prison. His Bible and books were taken from him. Erelong came his day in court. The following account is abbreviated from the report given by E. E. Andross, president of the Inter-American Division:

"Sternly the judge demanded to know what this man was teaching. The evangelist saw his own Bible on the court desk, and asked permission to read his teaching from the Holy Scriptures. He read the ten commandments, as spoken by the voice of God. As he began to read the words of that holy law, he noticed the judge's countenance change. He was looking intently beyond and above our evangelist's head. There was an expression of startled fear on his face as the reading of God's law continued.

"When the reader stopped, the judge's eyes were removed from the object of his intent gaze, and were turned in questioning to the prisoner. 'Who is the man who came in with you? And where has he gone?' the judge asked. 'No one was with me,' replied the accused. 'Yes, there was some one, taller than you, who stood behind you looking at me as you read,' said the judge. 'But he is gone!' And turning to the police officer, the magistrate directed that the evangelist be set free, and be no more interfered with."

"Where Are Your Watchmen?"

In the earliest days of missions in the East Indies, in 1856, Von Asselt was pioneering in the wilds of Sumatra. At times the missionary and his wife were so conscious, night after night, of encircling danger from fierce head-hunting tribesmen that they could maintain their courage only by pleading the promises of God. After two years, when they had moved to a more quiet place, they had a visit one day from men of the region where they had first pitched their camp. The missionary tells of the visiting chief's request:

"Finally he began: 'Now, tuan [teacher], I have yet one request.'

" 'And what is that?'

" 'I would like to have a closer look at your watchmen.'

" 'What watchmen do you mean? I do not have any.'

" 'I mean the watchmen whom you station around your house at night, to protect you.'

" 'But I have no watchmen,' I said again; 'I have only a little herdboy and a little cook, and they would make poor watchmen.'

"Then the man looked at me incredulously, as if he wished to say: 'O, do not try to make me believe otherwise, for I know better.'

"Then he asked: 'May I look through your house, to see if they are hid there?'

" 'Yes, certainly,' I said, laughing; 'look through it; you will not find anybody.' So he went in and searched in every corner, even through the beds, but came to me very much disappointed.

"Then I began a little probing myself, and requested him to tell me the circumstances under which he saw those watchmen of whom he spoke."

.The chief told how, again and again, in the first days of the mission, he and his men had come by night to burn the mission and kill the missionary. But they found watchmen on guard. They then hired a professional assassin to do the deed. He boasted of no fear of any watchman, and went forward to do the work. But back he came, running, saying that he found watchmen standing shoulder to shoulder, whose weapons "shine like fire."

" 'But now, tell me, tuan, who are those watchmen? Have you never seen them?'

" 'No, I have never seen them.'

" 'And your wife did not see them?'

" 'No, my wife did not see them.'

" 'But yet we have all seen them; how is that?'

"Then I went in and brought a Bible from our house, and holding it open before him, said:

" 'See here; this book is the word of our great God, in which He promises to guard and defend us, and we firmly believe that word; therefore we need not to see the watchmen: but you do not believe; therefore the great God has to show you the watchmen, in order that you may learn to believe.' "

The Indian's Confession

Somewhat similar to the early experience in Sumatra was one that came to our missionary in a new outpost in the high Andes of South America. The Indians were fanatically fearful of the mission. They were constantly threatening it. On three nights, particularly, the mission family saw signs of gathering hostility. But they could only pray. And then the situation turned for the better, and they began to gain the confidence of the mountain people. Then, at last, a friendly Indian was converted. He told the story of those nights of threatening. Made brief, the Indian's story was, in substance:

"They feared the mission would bring calamity upon them. They decided to destroy it. Coming up one night to do the deed, they found watchmen at the door. Thinking that somehow word of the plan that night had reached the family, they

3

decided to defer the attack. Next night they came again, but found more guards, all about the house. Now, they said, we shall have to have more men. We will gather a big enough force to rush these watchmen and finish the job. So a great force was gathered, armed with all kinds of weapons and implements. In the dead of night the attackers mustered and came over the rise looking down upon the mission. Then, lo! they saw a sight that affrighted every one. Soldiers were marching in about the mission—hundreds of them. They were armed, and marched in military order. Terrified, the attackers fled for their lives."

That was the explanation of those nights when a sense of danger led the mission family to special prayer. And well the family knew that not a watchman—a human watchman—had been on the place, and not a soldier within many a mile.

At the Raging River

In the early days of South African missions, Missionary Lange and his wife had to flee by ox team from a Kafir uprising. Their daughter, the late Mrs. Blaine, one of our veteran members, told me in Africa the story of deliverance at a raging river. "I have heard my mother tell it often," she said. When the fleeing party came to the river, they found it had "come down" in one of those sudden floods. "It is of no use," the drivers said. The river was full from brim to brim. Mrs. Blaine said:

"My mother was ill, and could not be moved from the wagon. There they were, in the rain and the gathering darkness, with the Kafirs on the warpath behind, and the torrent closing the way of escape. The native boys were in terror, and the oxen very nearly unmanageable. My parents could only lift their hearts to God for help.

"Just then, my mother said, two black men stepped up, and in a calm and forceful voice said, 'Do you want to cross over the river?'

" 'Yes,' said my mother; 'we must sleep at Umdushani's kraal tonight. But the river is so full we cannot cross.'

" 'We will take you over,' said the men.

"They asked my mother to sit perfectly still. Then these men took charge, quieted the frightened oxen, guided them into the river and across, and up the banks to safety on the other side. It was wonderful to those who saw it done. When the wagon stopped on the other side, my father and mother wanted to thank the men for what they had done; but they were gone! They had disappeared as suddenly as they had appeared at the critical moment. The native boys, who had come through on the wagon, had never seen the men before, and did not know where they came from, nor did they see them as they withdrew.

"It had all been so sudden, and quiet, and providential that my father and mother could see in it only the direct hand of Providence bringing deliverance as they called upon God for help. They soon reached Umdushani's kraal and safety."

Who can question the faith that led Mother Lange to say always: "Nothing will ever persuade me that God did not send His angels that night"?

The Companion on the Rocks

In the far Northland, on the Scandinavian peninsula, Colporteur Hokland made his way down the mountainside to reach families in the valley with his books. At one steep, dangerous place, he stopped to pray, asking God to send His angel to go with him. He safely reached the valley. The account goes:

"At the first cottage he met a man and his wife, who, it seems, had been watching him as he came over the mountain.

" 'What has become of your companion?' was their first question, after the ordinary salutation.

" 'What companion?' asked the missionary.

" 'The man who was with you.'

" 'But there was no one with me; I am alone.'

" 'Is that possible?' they exclaimed in surprise. 'We were watching you as you came, and it really seemed to us that there were two men crossing the mountain together.'

" 'Then,' reported Missionary Hokland, 'I was reminded of my prayer to God for help, and of the word of the Lord in Psalms . 34 :7, "The angel of the Lord encampeth round about them that fear Him, and delivereth them." ' "

The Japanese Inquirer

George Ensor, as a teacher, was first agent of the Church of England missions in Japan. He landed in 1869. Then the old bulletin boards still gave notice on the highways that Christianity was forbidden : "If any one is suspected, a report must be made at once." Mr. Ensor's rooms were watched. One dark night a young Japanese appeared at Ensor's door. "I wish to be a Christian," he said. Asked if he knew the peril of such a step, he replied:

"Yes, I know. Last night I came to your gate, and fear overpowered me, and I returned. But there stood by me in the night one who came to me in my dreams, and said I was to go to the house of the missionary and nothing would happen to me, and I have come." "And drawing his long sword," Mr. Ensor said, "he held it up to me in a form signifying the Japanese oath, and promised that he would ever keep true to me, and I received him."—*Stock's "History of the Church Missionary Society," Vol. II.*

In receiving this first convert into the church in Japan, Mr. Ensor renamed him Titus; "for God," he said, in Paul's words, "who comforteth those who are cast down, comforted me by the coming of Titus."

"A Mysterious Rescue"

So Missionary F. A. Stahl, pioneer in the Lake Titicaca missions, describes a deliverance that came in the early days, before thousands of these Indians around the lake had been changed by the gospel. Led on by priests, a great mob was attacking the mission, crying, "Pitchim catum!" (Catch them and burn them!) In his "Land of the Incas," the missionary says:

"At this juncture, the priests called loudly to the Indians to set fire to the straw roof; and soon some were coming with torches to obey the command. One of them climbed upon a pile of stones to light the roof; but as he applied the torch, the Indian woman who owned the hut jumped up on the stones beside him, knocking him off, and pulled out the burning straw with her hands. Just as she succeeded in tearing out the last of it, she fell down, and some of the straw fell upon her bare head, burning her severely. She afterward proved a very important witness, because of this.

"At this moment, when others of the Indians were making ready their torches to set fire to the hut, and we had given up all hope of rescue, the whole mob, priests and all, withdrew. We came out of the hut in time to see the priests mount their horses quickly, and flee across the valley, the mob following them.

"We asked a frightened-looking Indian who stood near, why these people had fled so precipitately. He said, 'Don't you see that great company of Indians coming, all armed, to defend you?' I did not see them. I turned to Mrs. Stahl, and asked her if she did. She said, 'No.' The Indian insisted that there was a great army of Indians coming to help us. We looked around, but could see no one. We know now that God sent His angels in that form to rescue us. There is no other way to account for what occurred."

A Companion in Trouble

In the early times of Methodism, a Welsh evangelist, John Jones, was riding by horse in a desolate part of northern Wales. He had considerable money with him. Approaching a place where he must dismount to open a gate, he saw a rough-looking man furtively running along behind the hedge, armed with a reaping hook. The minister prayed God for protection. Instantly a strange rider on a white horse appeared at his side. He says:

"I described to the stranger the dangerous position in which I had been placed, and how relieved I felt by his sudden appearance. He made no reply; and on looking at his face, I saw that he was intently gazing in the direction of the gate. I followed his gaze, and saw the reaper emerge from his concealment, and run across the field to our left. He had evidently seen that I was no longer alone, and had given up his intended attempt.

"All cause for alarm being now removed, I endeavored to enter into conversation with my deliverer, but again without the slightest success. Not a word did he give me in reply. I continued talking, however, as we rode toward the gate, though I utterly failed to see any reason for, and indeed felt rather hurt at, his silence. Only once did I hear his voice. Having watched the reaper disappear over the brow of a neighboring hill, I turned to my companion, and said, 'Can it for a moment be doubted that my prayer was heard, and that you were sent for my deliverance, by the Lord?' Then the horseman uttered the single word, 'Amen.' Not another word did he give, though I continued endeavoring to get from him replies to my questions, both in English and in Welsh. As we approached the gate I rode forward to open it. I turned to look, and—he was gone. He was nowhere to be seen. What could I then believe? But one thing, and that was that my prayer had been heard, and that help had indeed been sent me at a time of peril. Full of this thought, I dismounted, and throwing myself on my knees at the side of the road, offered up a prayer of thankfulness to Him who had so signally preserved me from danger.

"I then mounted my horse and continued on my journey. Through the years that have elapsed since that memorable July day, I have never for an instant wavered in the belief that I had a special providential deliverance."

The Fourth Man in the Boat

On a dangerous section of one of Venezuela's rivers, Missionary L. J. Borrowdale, of our Inter-American Division, had made his way safely over unknown waters. He and two companions knew that there had been moments of real peril. Later, returning over a better channel, they stopped at a house on the riverbank. The missionary says:

"The owner of the house wanted to know where our companion was. We told him he was down at the boat, and would soon be up. I thought he had reference to the boy.

"He asked, 'But where is the other one?' I said we were all there. He said that there had been four of us when we went up. He then asked, 'Didn't you know that this is a very dangerous part of the river?'

"We replied that we did not know that it was.

"Then he said, pointing to my companion, 'You were at the front steering, and you [pointing to me] were at the side leaning over to watch, and the boy was on the other side taking the depth of the river.'

"I asked, 'Where was the other man?'

"He replied, 'He was standing right by you.'

"He told us how each of us was dressed, and I asked, 'What did the other man have on?'

"He replied, 'He was dressed in white, and he stood beside you.'

"Later he told us the same thing again, and I was made to realize that 'the angel of the Lord encampeth round about them that fear Him, and delivereth them.' We should never forget to give God thanks, for many times He delivers us from dangers of which we are not aware."

The "Other Man" in the Storm

Two Mexican colporteurs, while making their way over a rough mountain road to a house where they were to stop, were caught at nightfall by a storm. The narrator says:

"A man came toward us on horseback; we could see him coming from quite a distance. As he came to us, we recognized him as one of our customers. Finally we arrived at our destination.

"The next morning we started on our march, and again we met the man that we had met the night before. This time he stopped and asked if we were not the same people that he had passed the evening before. We replied that we were. Then he said, 'But there was another man walking just ahead of you yesterday; where is he now?'

" 'Brother,' we replied, 'we know that it must have been the angel of the Lord with us, guiding the way through the storm.' "

Who Stopped Him?

On the great island of Trinidad in the South Caribbean, a colporteur was hurrying through a dense forest. M. E. Lowry, leader of our colporteur work in that field, writes:

"Suddenly the colporteur halted. He was stopped as quickly as if he had run up against a stone wall, though he could see no reason for it until he dropped his eyes to the path. Right there where his foot would have landed had he taken one step more, all coiled up and apparently sleeping, lay a large mapipire, Trinidad's most feared and venomous serpent. Thanking his heavenly Father for the fulfillment of His precious promise in Psalms 121:8 ('The Lord shall preserve thy going out and thy coming in'), he passed on with renewed courage."

"Between Me and Those Praying People Stood an Angel"

On the large island of Mindanao, part of the Philippine group, where Moslem, pagan, and Catholic influences furnish a field in which religious prejudices may easily flare into flame, a Filipino Bible worker was conducting meetings. "The husband of one woman attending," wrote L. O. Pattison, "became angry, and purposed to kill the worker." The man later told this story:

"I had fully made up my mind to go to the home of the Bible worker, and at the time of the meeting, when they were on their knees praying, to enter the room and slay the worker. So on the night of the meeting I went to the house with my bolo [a large knife] and waited at the door. After they had finished singing and had knelt to pray, I stepped into the room, fully intent on beheading the leader of that company. But I was dumfounded. There, between me and those praying people, stood an angel with his wings outspread! I turned and ran in fright to my own home and locked myself in."

"HE DELIVERETH AND RESCUETH"

*"He worketh signs and wonders in heaven and in earth."
Dan. 6:27.*

Daniel in the Lions' Den

THE story of Daniel in the lions' den—how it has filled hearts with trust in God, from infancy to old age! King Darius, of Babylon, after fasting all night, repenting of his weakness, came trembling in the morning and cried down into the den:

"O Daniel, servant of the living God, is thy God, whom thou servest continually, able to deliver thee from the lions?"

And from down in the den, where the lions paced to and fro or crouched before the servant of God, there came the comforting response:

"O king, live forever. My God hath sent His angel, and hath shut the lions' mouths, that they have not hurt me: forasmuch as before Him innocency was found in me."

No wonder the king issued the proclamation declaring the God of Daniel the true and living God who "delivereth and rescueth."

Savage Beasts Restrained

Many a missionary, seemingly at the mercy of wild beasts, has drawn trust from the story of Daniel and the lions, and has felt the consciousness of the restraining power of the angels.

Mrs. Scudder, of India, hearing that her husband, Dr. John Scudder, medical missionary, was sick in the jungle, hired bearers and started to go to him. In the night the tigers roared so terribly that the bearers dropped their loads and fled, leaving her alone. The missionary annals say:

"With no human arm to protect her, the defenseless woman spent the long hours of that lonely night in prayer. Again and again she heard the tread of wild elephants, and the low, menacing growls of tigers not far away. 'All night long,' says her brother, 'they seemed to be circling around the spot where she knelt, ready to spring upon her and her child. But God held them back.'

"In the morning the bearers returned, and the journey was resumed. At its close, Mrs. Scudder found the crisis past and her husband convalescent."

A woman colporteur, carrying our truth-filled books to homes in the Southwestern United States, has left on record this account:

"I was in a country district. As I came up through the yard to a house, a dog with a chain dangling from his neck rushed savagely at me. He was just ready to attack and bite me when he seemed seized with fright. He gave one yelp of terror, and ran back under the house to hide away. Just at that instant the lady came excitedly to the door and said, 'Oh, did the dog bite you?'

" 'No,' I replied, 'he seemed frightened at me.'

" 'Frightened!' she answered. 'No. He was not frightened. He is terribly savage. We cannot allow him at large when strangers are about. My husband let him loose this morning because I was to be left alone at home.'

" 'Well,' I said, 'then the angel of the Lord must have frightened him, because I did not touch him when he rushed at me.'

" 'That is more like it,' the lady said, 'for I know you could never have come up to this door without a miracle from heaven.' "

A young colporteur attacked by a savage dog sent up a prayer to God. The beast had reared up to spring for his throat, but fell back dead. From every continent, members of the great colporteur army have sent reports of deliverances from fierce beasts as the worker's heart was lifted in prayer to the God of Daniel.

Inquirers Directed, Messengers Prepared to Answer

The Roman officer at Cæsarea, a seeker after God, was directed by a dream to send men to Joppa, to bring one Simon Peter to teach him the way of salvation. And while the men were on the road, Peter in Joppa was prepared by a dream to respond to the call. Acts 10. It was an important turn in the early days of the gospel work among the Gentiles.

In the early days of the advent movement a young school teacher of Massachusetts was urged by her Adventist mother to attend a Sabbath meeting. The mother was praying earnestly for the daughter. "Just to please my mother I'll go," Miss Smith said to herself. But that Friday night she dreamed of the meeting place, and of the speaker, and of the topic, "Unto two thousand and three hundred days, then shall the sanctuary be cleansed."

That same Friday night Joseph Bates, who was to be the speaker that Sabbath, in a dream saw the meeting place, which he had never visited. He saw the congregation, and saw a young woman enter, whose name was spoken to him in the dream, "Annie R. Smith." He saw in the dream that she would accept the message of truth.

Sabbath morning came, and Joseph Bates rose to speak. He was not thinking of his dream until the young woman whom he had seen in the dream entered the room before his eyes. He recognized her at once. He had chosen a certain topic, but seemed forced to change, and spoke from the text, "Unto two thousand and three hundred days, then shall the sanctuary be cleansed," setting forth the advent message of Revelation 14, and the Sabbath reform.

At the close of the service Joseph Bates greeted the young lady by name, saying, "I dreamed of seeing you last night." "Then Annie told her dream," says J. N. Loughborough (in "The Great Second Advent Movement"). "She left the meeting with feelings and aspirations all changed, having there and then accepted the truth." Her short life was a blessing to our early publishing work; and still we sing her hymn of the advent hope and the heavenly home:

> "Not far from home! O blessed thought!
> The traveler's lonely heart to cheer;
> Which oft a healing balm has brought,
> And dried the mourner's tear.

Then weep no more, since we shall meet
Where weary footsteps never roam—
Our trials past, our joys complete,
Safe in our Father's home."

"Arise Up Quickly"—Go!

The angel of the Lord came into Herod's prison, wakened the apostle Peter from sound sleep, put the spirit of deep sleep upon his guards, and said to him in a commanding voice that only he heard, "Arise up quickly!" It seemed only a dream to Peter—until he was left alone and free in the street outside the prison, the night air blowing on his face. Of the lesson for our day in these experiences of ancient time, we are told:

"To the worker for God, the record of these angel visits should bring strength and courage. Today, as verily as in the days of the apostles, heavenly messengers are passing through the length and breadth of the land, seeking to comfort the sorrowing, to protect the impenitent, to win the hearts of men to Christ. We cannot see them personally; nevertheless they are with us, guiding, directing, protecting."— *"The Acts of the Apostles," by Ellen G. White, pp. 152, 153.*

"Get up and go!" a voice at midnight cried to a young Chinese medical missionary.

In 1926, young Doctor ——, of South China, was captured by bandits, who held him prisoner in a cave for ransom. Of his second night in captivity, Missionary I. B. Newcomb wrote:

"He claimed the promises of Psalms 34:4, 7, and that evening went to sleep, feeling assured that the Lord would not forsake him.

"About midnight he was awakened by some one's telling him, 'Get up and go!' At first he thought the men were joking with him. He spoke to them, but they were all sound asleep. He quickly arose and slipped out past the two men on guard at the entrance, who were sleeping soundly.

"He started to run, but where should he run? Here he was, miles from he didn't know where. So as he ran he breathed a short prayer for guidance, and immediately heard the same voice that told him to get out, now telling him, 'Follow the stars.' On looking up, he saw three very bright stars shining through the clouds that covered the sky elsewhere. These he followed as he ran, stumbling and falling over the boulders (he afterward showed me many bruises and cuts he had received on the jagged rocks), until he arrived at a small village on a river, where he secured lodging for the remainder of the night, and the next morning took a boat for home."

In Leeuwarden prison, in Reformation times, a Protestant girl, Hadewyck, was awaiting trial for her faith, and possible death. Elizabeth, her friend, had just been tortured by thumbscrews, and then tied in a sack and drowned in the canal. As Hadewyck prayed, she heard her name called. She could see no one, and resumed her prayer. A second time she heard the call, and a third time, now the voice saying, "Hadewyck, I tell you to depart!" Then, says the old Dutch martyrology of the Baptists, Hadewyck rose and looked about her. "Seeing the door open, she put on her cloak and went out of the prison." She made her escape, with further providential experiences, and lived to work many years for God.

Prayer and Praise in Prison

Two New Testament evangelists were in prison, feet fast in the stocks, and backs smarting from the lashes laid upon them. "And at midnight Paul and Silas prayed, and sang praises unto God: and the prisoners heard them." Acts 16:25. Out of that midnight service of prayer and praise, the mighty arm of Providence sent deliverance.

In Southeastern Europe two colporteur evangelists, joyful successors of Paul and Silas, were carrying books to the people, teaching the same old gospel of salvation. The priests made charges that they were dangerous communists. That was sufficient to throw them into prison without inquiry or trial. The cell was damp and cold, but with warm and thankful hearts they began to pray and sing the songs of Zion.

"It so happened," we are told, "that some gentlemen of influence passed that way. They were astonished to hear songs of praise and the voice of prayer coming from the barred prison window. They stopped and listened. Then they went to the authorities.

" 'Who are these prisoners?' they asked.

" 'They are two dangerous communists that we have arrested, charged by the priest.'

" 'Nonsense,' said the gentlemen. 'These men are no communists. You never heard of a communist singing hymns and praying to God.'

"So insistent were these influential men that the official set our brethren free, and the men who had intervened provided them a supper and a good room and beds. The colporteurs next day went on their way rejoicing."

Their Eyes Were Held

In defiance of the living God, the king of the Syrians sent a band of soldiers to take the prophet Elisha. They had the prophet surrounded on a hill. Elisha prayed to God, "Smite this people, I pray Thee, with blindness." And the blinded troops were led into the camp of Israel, where their eyes were opened and a feast was spread for them. Then they were allowed to go, with sufficient evidence that Syria was fighting against the living God. (See 2 Kings 6.)

In the early mission story of South Africa, a Kafir war party had threatened Missionary George Brown. Finally, in exhaustion, Brown gave up trying to hide and escape. He sat down on a rock by the stream Keiskamma:

"There I sat," he said, "exposed to every eye. Bands of excited men passed within less than twenty yards. There was not an intervening bush to hide me from them. Yet group after group passed by, never looking at me. Surely that Jehovah to whom Elisha prayed, 'Smite this people, I pray Thee, with blindness,' was not far from me that day!"

The same hostile bands, he learned later, had killed many foreigners that day, while he, a missionary, was apparently hidden from their sight. His Kafir helper said to him: "Do you now see that it was God only this day?"

"I did not see them!" cried a would-be assassin in Spain. The late Evangelist F. Bond, a pioneer in our work in Spain, told how a man with a fancied grievance came to a train the evangelist was known to be taking, armed to kill him. But though some minutes before the train started the evangelist and two friends had passed him on the platform, he did not see them. "I did not see them! I did not see them!" he cried out, as the train began to move, and he then saw the man he meant to attack. "Later I met the man," said the evangelist. "He believed the Lord had restrained him that day, and this conviction had cooled his anger. He believed God had mercifully hindered and he was thoroughly repentant."

During the World War one of our Armenian evangelists was endeavoring to cross Asia Minor to reach safety in Syria and Egypt; for Christian Armenians were being sent to prison or exile or death. On the train to Damascus, police were inspecting passengers, demanding passports. The evangelist had none. He says:

"When the policeman had finished with the first coach, I tried to enter there. I was unable to enter it, and also the second. I had to go back to my own third carriage. I kept just behind the policeman as he passed from seat to seat, praying in my heart that he might not be allowed to notice me. How strange that so simple an expedient could be successful! As he passed along I sat down in a place where he had already looked. He did not see me, and I was saved. It meant my very life."

He got to Damascus, where his wife joined him. But orders were issued to arrest the Armenians who had no passes. Soldiers searched the houses. "At least twenty-five times those searching parties came to our street," said the evangelist. "They searched the houses on each side of us, but they never came to ours. It seemed a miracle. Two years we lived there."

"How do you account for it?" the evangelist was asked.

"Well, you remember how the Lord, at Elisha's prayer, held the eyes of the men of Syria," he replied. "That is the only way I can account for it."

Sent to a Praying Home

Long ago a convicted sinner was praying for help in Damascus. The word of the Lord came to one of His servants in that city:

"Arise, and go into the street which is called Straight, and inquire in the house of Judas for one called Saul, of Tarsus: for, behold, he prayeth." Acts 9:11.

Heaven knows the streets of all the cities, and the homes and hearts praying for light; and angels rejoice to guide the gospel worker to the praying ones.

Years ago, Evangelist B. C. Tabor, of Oregon, told me this story of a praying home in one town. He said:

"In working from house to house in the town, I had noticed a house that stood apart in a field, at some distance from the street along which I often passed at a late afternoon hour on the way to my stopping place. I felt I should go to that house, but my hands were more than full of work, and in the weariness and pressure I put it off. But the conviction still came as I passed that way, returning from the day's work.

"When I had delayed for three weeks, I felt I must go, and I went across the field and knocked at the door. A woman opened the door, and I saw that she had been weeping. I showed her the tracts that I had been circulating, and spoke of the study of the Bible.

" 'Friend,' she said, looking intently at me, 'the Lord sent you here. For three weeks I have been praying at this hour for light. God sent you to me.' She accepted the light of truth with a glad heart."

For three weeks she had prayed; for three weeks the Christian worker had felt the impression that he must go to that house.

ANCIENTLY the Lord used the "burning bush"—shining with a light that was not fire—to secure the attention of Moses and make clear to him that he was divinely called into a life of service.

The Lighted Commandment

Our story of progress in the Philippines affords many an illustration of providential working to call men's attention to the truth. In early times a Filipino pastor came to our headquarters in Manila from a far province. He told this story, reported by Director L. V. Finster:

"One of his members had come to him impressed by a dream in which he had seen a dove descend from heaven and alight upon the fourth commandment. A bright glory shone out from that text of Scripture. The pastor said, 'It may be that the Lord has light for us in that commandment.' So they began to study their Bible. After a while the member said, 'Why, this scripture says the seventh day is the Sabbath, and we are keeping the first day instead.' They began to search other parts of the Bible, and erelong were convinced that the seventh day should be kept; that the Lord had never given instruction for the keeping of Sunday. Then it was that the pastor of the little congregation came all the long distance to Manila to get help. He spent a week in study, and went back to preach the second coming of Christ and the call of Sabbath reform to his people."

A Flame That Did Not Burn

The merely strange and unusual may mean nothing vital. But when experiences out of the ordinary are used to bring forth fruits of obedience to God and trust in the sure founda-

4

tion of Holy Scripture, we may recognize the interposition of Providence. In the organ of our South American Division, the *Bulletin,* of Buenos Aires, Conrad Aeschlimann, an evangelist, tells how a man of the Greek Orthodox Catholic Church was led into the light. The man had been interested in public meetings held there. One day the evangelist visited him. The man said, "I hope you will explain something to me." Then this inquirer told how he had been awakened in the night and found a light shining among the books that lay on the table. He said:

"Naturally, my first impression was that a fire had been started. But on examining the thing I found the light came from my Bible. I observed the phenomenon for quite a time. It disappeared only when I turned on the light."

Later, he had again seen the light. The people in whose house he had a room—a Jewish family—thought his experience one of illusion. But when the light was seen again in the darkness of night, he called the family.

"What was their surprise," he related, "to see it with their own eyes. They examined everything, even to taking the Bible in their hands, but the light remained. Their surprise was even greater when they touched the flame and it did not burn them. Upon the turning on of the lights in the room the light about the Book disappeared. Now, what is the meaning of this thing?"

The evangelist assured the inquirer that the Lord apparently had given him this experience to lead him to study the Bible and receive its teaching as real light for his heart and soul. More earnestly than ever the man gave himself to such study, and not again was the experience repeated. Evidently no further visible sign was needed to impress him with the importance of following the light of the word. "The brother was convinced," says the evangelist, "that the experience was a call from God. He is keeping the commandments of God and preparing for baptism. God has many ways of bringing His truth to His own."

A Light From Above

With this experience from Argentina, we may put the following story from Brazil, reported thus by O. Montgomery after a visit to South America:

" 'God moves in a mysterious way, His wonders to perform.' His divine providence, the evidences of His love and power, are many times manifested in a remarkable manner in the dark corners of the earth, to open the hearts of those who have never known His truth, to the light of His word.

"Brother Leo Halliwell, superintendent of the Lower Amazon Mission, tells of the conversion of the sister of Brother Michiles, our first believer in Maués River country. This good woman was greatly stirred because her brother had become a Seventh-day Adventist and was keeping the seventh day of the week as the Sabbath. He defended his new faith so strongly from the Bible that the sister felt she must secure a Bible for the purpose of combating the truth and showing her brother wherein he was wrong. When she had succeeded in getting a Bible, she gathered her daughters about her, and they sat down to read the word of God with the idea of finding something with which she could convince her brother of his error.

"Suddenly a bright and wonderful light shone through the roof of the house into their very presence, though there was no opening in the roof. They all saw the light, and were greatly astonished, and filled with fear. The mother said to her daughters, 'Surely this is the word of God.' They immediately began to study the Bible in search of the truth, rather than for the purpose of fighting the truth. The Lord enlightened them by the word, and in a little time the entire family were rejoicing in this wonderful message, and were united with Brother Michiles in the observance of the Sabbath of the Lord."

A Thankful Japanese Listener

An elderly Japanese woman who came into an evangelist's meeting had her attention riveted upon the preacher and his message by an uncommon experience. She could not read. Later she came to feel that in her ignorance God had in mercy drawn her attention to the Christian teaching by special means. After she had destroyed her idols and become fully a Christian, she told this experience, reported by Evangelist Kuniya:

"When I came to the meeting the first night, I had never heard a Christian sermon. As I came into the meeting room with my daughter, and sat down, there seemed to be a strange light by you while you were speaking.

"I asked my daughter if she could see it; but she said that she could see nothing strange. I continued to see it as long as you were speaking from the Bible; and since I have learned more of the Bible, I have come to believe that this light that stood by you must have been an angel of the Lord sent to lead me to the true religion. I thank and praise Him for showing the light to me, a poor heathen."

The Book That Was Not Consumed

It was in Czechoslovakia, the land of Huss, the Reformer, that a Bible passed through the fire unscathed, to the joy of a praying wife. The mother and daughter had become Adventists, but in that Catholic region the husband was bitterly opposed to their faith. President H. F. Schuberth, of Central Europe, told the story as follows:

"One afternoon when some of our people were visiting there, the husband took the Bible, the New Testament, 'His Glorious Appearing,' and some papers, and put them in the kitchen stove, and was very happy when the fire was burning well. Oar poor sisters were crying at the loss of their good books and papers. At suppertime, when our sister went to make the fire again, in taking out the ashes she felt something hard. She looked closely, and there she found the Bible and the New Testament! They were not burned at all! All the other books and papers were burned to ashes, but the Bible looked just as nice as if it had never been in the fire. Today that husband is no more angry with his wife. When church time comes, he says, 'It's time for you to go now.'"

Amazon Waters Could Not Quench the Light

This is not a story of visible light, but of spiritual light from the sacred page, that even all the wide Amazon flood could not quench. Missionary Halliwell, of the Lower Amazon, reports:

"In the beginning of the year 1930 the Meyer church of Rio de Janeiro sent a leather-bound Bible to the Indians of the first Indian school organized in the Lower Amazon Mission, at a place called Cinco Kilos. The Bible was presented to the chief by Superintendent Wilcox. After a brief visit the brethren returned to the city of Maués in the mission launch 'Mensageiro' (Messenger). After the departure of the brethren, a man who was very much opposed to our work took the Bible from the Indian chief, tore off the cover, and then began to tear the leaves out one by one and throw them in the river.

"The work in this village made little progress for some time after this incident. We had to take our teacher away, and the Indians themselves moved to other villages. The pages of the Bible, however, that were thrown on the water, were like seeds of truth carried to all parts of the country. The story of the torn book soon spread, and today we have over four hundred Sabbathkeepers, living all along this one short tributary of the Amazon. One Sabbath school has more than one hundred members."

"THOU ART MY KING, O GOD: COMMAND DELIVERANCES" (Ps. 44:4)

"We have heard with our ears, O God, our fathers have told us, what work Thou didst in their days, in the times of old." Ps. 44:1.

The Walls Fell Down

"By faith the walls of Jericho fell down, after they were compassed about seven days." Heb. 11:30. Angels that excel in strength must have laid hold upon those walls. Joshua 6:20.

Foxe tells of a Protestant, Williamson, imprisoned in Queen Mary's days. He seemed to hear a voice, "Arise, and go thy ways." He hesitated, and again it spoke. He gave himself to earnest prayer; and the third time the voice spoke. "So he arising upon the same," says the old chronicler, "immediately a piece of the prison wall fell down!" While the officers were coming in at the front gate Williamson leaped out over the opened wall and escaped.

In earlier days of our work in Peru, Evangelists Howell and Howard with an Indian helper were invited into a certain street in a fanatically Catholic village. They found it to be a dead-end street, blocked by a house. On each side was a high wall. Then a mob armed with stones came down the street following them, crying, "Kill the heretics!" The only thing they could do was to try to ride through the mob. Small hope there was of that. But as the missionaries spurred their horses toward the approaching crowd, a portion of the wall was seen to have just fallen. The fallen stones lay rolled in the street, and could not have been there as they rode in. "I turned my horse and went through the opening," says Missionary J. M. Howell, "and Brother Howard and the Indian followed." Thus they escaped from the fury of the angry mob, "thankful to God for His protection in" their hour of need.

Protected by Dissensions Among the Adversaries

The Roman commander at Jerusalem wished to learn what crime the Jewish leaders charged against Paul. He summoned the leaders in council and permitted the apostle to speak to them. Paul appealed to the Pharisees on his faith in the resurrection:

"Of the hope and resurrection of the dead I am called in question. And when he had so said, there arose a dissension between the Pharisees and the Sadducees [who denied a resurrection]: and the multitude was divided." Acts 23:6, 7.

There was such a "great cry" and tumult among themselves that the Roman officer could readily see that it was controversy about belief and not a matter of crime or any evil deed that Paul had committed; so he rescued Paul from his fighting adversaries.

It was in ancient Asia that the apostle Paul found safety in the violent dissension that arose between the differing schools of Pharisees and Sadducees. In modern Asia, in early prewar days, an Armenian Seventh-day Adventist evangelist, the late Z. G. Baharian, found deliverance by dissensions that arose between members of a mob seeking his life. The building where he had held a meeting was surrounded. Stones were flying. He wrote:

"Death seemed very near. We had no refuge but God, whom we trusted. One man was climbing up the wall to enter and take me out. If I were once in their hands, I could have no hope for life. But surely the angels of God had been sent to keep me from danger. I prayed to God, holding fast to His word, and, behold, the people became divided, one class saying, 'Let us take him out this very night,' and the other, 'Let us wait till tomorrow.' The latter prevailed, and they went home, leaving everything very still. For this we rejoiced, and thanked God."

Delivered From Serpents

When the barbarian people on ancient Malta saw a viper fasten its fangs in Paul's hand, as he helped to gather wood for the fire, they thought his death sure. "No doubt," they said, "this man is a murderer, whom, though he hath escaped the sea, yet vengeance suffereth not to live." But when he shook the serpent into the fire, and went on about his work, suffering no harm, "they changed their minds, and said that he was a god." Acts 28:3-6. This deliverance prepared them for the ministry of Paul among them, and no doubt opened the way for gospel work on Malta later, as all this Mediterranean field was covered by the labors of the apostolic church.

In the early Moravian mission days, the missionary Dahne had a station up the Corentyn River, in the Guianas of South America. One evening as he was in the hut, a great boa (a serpent that crushes and swallows its prey) swung down from a shelf and drew its coils about him. He wrestled until exhausted. Feeling death certain, he feared that people who should find him gone would think his native Indians had killed him, and so be prejudiced against them. One hand was free, and he got near the table and wrote with a piece of chalk on the boards, "A serpent has killed me." Then, suddenly, the text came to him, "They shall take up serpents." Mark 16:18. "Seizing the creature with great force," he says, "I tore it loose and flung it out of the hut. I then lay down to rest in the peace of God."

Deliverance by Earthquake

As Paul and Silas were shut in the Roman prison, held fast in the stocks, their hearts the meanwhile full of such joy in Christ that they sang praises at midnight, "suddenly there was a great earthquake, so that the foundations of the prison were shaken: and immediately all the doors were opened, and every one's bands were loosed." Acts 16:26.

The shaking earth meant deliverance to the evangelists and the conversion of the keeper and all his house.

During the World War, thousands of Armenian Christians were done to death by persecution in Asia Minor. One man, who was baptized by our mission in Constantinople just after the war, told Director H. Erzberger how he came through those times.

"You will probably ask me," he said, " 'How is it you and your little brother have been spared alive?' We must reply, It is because God intervened and delivered us miraculously."

Then he told how the exile party which he was in, being driven into the mountains, were suddenly surrounded by Kurds and the guards. "All," he said, "were armed with rifles or weapons of other sort. The bloody attack began. Women and children wailed, and men shuddered. Soon the cries of despair turned to loud supplication. All fell to the ground and began to utter fervent prayers to God. And God intervened. There was a terrible earthquake. The ground trembled and cracked beneath our feet. It was too evident a sign to our attackers that our cries had ascended to the throne of God. Perplexed and terrified, they left us and went away."

Not many, this narrator said, who had vowed faithfulness to God in the hour of peril, maintained that spirit after deliverance came. But he himself did not forget. He wanted more light, and found it among some of our refugee believers in Syria.

Stoned and Left for Dead; but Immediately to the Work Again

The opposing Jews from Antioch persuaded the heathen people at Lystra that Paul should be killed, "and having stoned Paul, drew him out of the city, supposing he had been dead. Howbeit, as the disciples stood round about him, he rose up, and came into the city: and the next day he departed with Barnabas to Derbe." Acts 14:19, 20.

The blessing of God gave healing and strength for immediate service, to the evangelist mourned as dead by those who gathered about him.

One of our European evangelists in a Greek Catholic country held a meeting. Afterward a mob attacked him with stones and clubs, leaving him unconscious. "A man came with a pitchfork," says President A. V. Olson, of the Southern European Division, "and wished to stab him. A voice cried out, 'Leave him alone! he is already dead.' The attackers drove away others of the believers, and the mob scattered.

"Then the evangelist came to consciousness and sat up. The stones were lying in heaps all about him. His little daughter now came, covered with bruises, and bleeding, for she had been struck. The evangelist rose up, and they started for home, accompanied by friends. The priest's wife, before whose door the attack had been made, saw the little party move away and cried out, 'Are you going to keep Sunday now?' The believers, we are told, covered with blood but joyful, went on their way to a town eighteen kilometers distant, singing one of their hymns, 'On Golgotha's hill took place the wondrous deed.' "

Warned by a Dream to Flee

King Herod plotted to slay all the infants in the coasts of Bethlehem, in order to kill the child Jesus, whose birth had been reported to him by the inquiring Wise Men of the East. It was at the direct instigation of Satan, watching to put Christ to death as soon as He should be born. Rev. 12:4. But Heaven sent a warning to Joseph in a dream by night to flee with the child and His mother into Egypt. Matt. 2:13. The armed searchers did not find them at Bethlehem.

A priest plotted to take captive all the members of our church in one town of Southeastern Europe. They were to be taken at one stroke, as they met on Sabbath. He had arranged on Friday for soldiers to surround the meeting place next morning. But he suddenly died that Friday night in his chair at home. The fear of God fell on the town as the people heard of it. "It is not good to persecute these people," they said to one another. But the soldiers had their orders. The believers told me how deliverance came:

"On Sabbath morning, however, the soldiers and police were at the meeting place, as they had been ordered, to arrest the Adventist worshipers. But there were none in the accustomed place of meeting that Sabbath morning.

"The Friday evening before, the elder of the little church had been warned in a dream not to meet that Sabbath in the usual place. So he had gathered the congregation elsewhere."

To the first conference session following the war, believers came in from that church, and reported that the work in their city was moving forward with the evident blessing and converting power of God.

A GUIDING VOICE FROM HEAVEN

"Thine ears shall hear a word behind thee, saying, This is the way, walk ye in it." Isa. 30:21.

In Lands of the Bible Story

SOMETIMES, in olden days, the Spirit spoke the message: "Then the Spirit said unto Philip, Go near, and join thyself to this chariot." Acts 8:29.

Often it was an angel who spoke: "Behold, the angel that talked with me went forth, and another angel went out to meet him, and said unto him, Run, speak to this young man." Zech. 2:3, 4.

In this same region of the eastern Mediterranean, one of our Armenian evangelists was holding meetings. There were often warm disputings, particularly from members of the Greek Catholic Church. The experience of a young Greek was thus related:

"This young Greek had been a quiet listener all the time, and when he heard the subject of the sanctuary and of Christ's ministry as our high priest, he embraced the truth. Hereupon he asked the brethren if they had ever heard him dispute. They told him they had not. He then explained why. 'The first time I came into your meeting,' he said, 'a voice said to me, "That young man has the truth. Listen to him; do not dispute!" And I followed the instructions of that voice; that is the reason I have not disputed.' "

Yet again in those times the Lord intervened in the unusual way. We are told:

"Another Greek was induced to come to the meeting. He opposed all that he heard, and finally decided not to come any more. One day, as he was crossing the street, a voice said, 'Turn down this street!' He said, 'No!' But the impression became so strong that he finally yielded, and turned down the street. As he arrived before the house in which our meeting was held, the voice spoke to him, 'Enter here,' and he said

58

again, 'I will not go into that meeting today!' But the Spirit strove with him until he went in."

Still the young man opposed and disputed; but on a journey shortly after, into ancient Cappadocia, the same Spirit that sent conviction into hearts in apostolic days strove with the young man until there on his journey he made his new surrender to Christ and to obedience to the truth.

"Akersgaten, 74"

This is a story of Oslo, Norway. Mrs. O——, who told me in California of the experience, had been a Lutheran. But having lost her mother, she was searching for some way of spiritual comfort and assurance, different from what she seemed to find in the church of her childhood. To this end, in Oslo, she had attended Sunday evening mass in a Catholic church which stands high at the head of the street called Akersgaten. She told me:

"As I came out of the church I heard a voice say, 'Akersgaten, 74.' I looked about to see who had said it. No one was in sight. I started down the long flight of stone steps. Again, midway, a voice spoke, 'Akersgaten, 74.' I stopped and looked back, thinking perhaps some nuns were talking. There was no one. Again, at the bottom of the steps the voice repeated, 'Akersgaten, 74.' Wondering, I thought I would watch for that number as I walked down Akersgaten. But in a moment I was past the Lutheran church on that street, and noticed the house numbers were in the 80's. I turned back, and on the corner, just across from the Catholic Church, I found the number '74.' On the second floor there seemed to be some gathering, and I heard singing. 'Very likely it's a club,' I thought, 'or some entertainment.' But I stepped up to the entrance to the hall and pushed the door open just a bit to glance in. Some one inside swung the door wide open and invited me in. There I heard my first Seventh-day Adventist sermon, which sent conviction to my heart."

Thus strangely guided, Mrs. O—— continued attending, and has since been a worker in the advent movement.

To the Pioneer of New Guinea

James Chalmers, pioneer of New Guinea missions, was seeking a site for a station in the wilds of the Fly River district. He anchored his cutter in the mouth of a creek. He says:

"It was an anxious night, as we did not know how we should be fixed in the morning. I did not know the creek, and there was only swampland about, and I wondered where the sandy land was that I had seen the year before. We had prayer, and I told Maru and his wife to stay by the boat, and that I would go and look around.

"I was very cast down. When walking along, I heard a voice very distinctly say to me, 'This is the way, walk ye in it.'

"I sat down on a log close by, and said, 'If Thine, O Lord, is the voice, teach me to hear and act;' and I heard, 'Fear not, for I am with thee; neither be thou dismayed.' I thanked God and took courage."

And it turned out to be the right place. The wild people gave him friendly welcome.

The Voice in the Tiger Jungle

The Godavari River, in south central India, was in flood. Dr. Jacob Chamberlain, a pioneer of that region, was caught out with a party, having expected to find a government boat on the river. Word came that the boat had broken down fighting the swift current. There seemed nothing for it but to hasten to higher land back from the river. It was a perilous way. Night would soon come, and already the roar of tigers could be heard in the jungles. The coolie carriers deserted their loads, and fled on for safety before the night should fall.

The missionary dropped back a bit from his marching party, to be alone with God. "Master," he prayed, "was it not for Thy sake we came here? Didst Thou not promise, 'I will be with thee'? . . . O Master, show me what to do!" In an old book, "In the Tiger Jungle," he tells how the answer came:

"An answer came, not audible, but distinct as though spoken in my ear by human voice: 'Turn to the left, to the Godavari, and you will find rescue.'

"Riding rapidly forward, I overtook the guides.

" 'How far is it to the Godavari?'

" 'A good mile.'

" 'Is there no village on its banks?'

" 'No, none within many miles, and the banks are all overflowed.'

" 'Is there no mound, no rising ground, on which we could camp, out of this water?

" 'It is all low and flat like this.'

"I drew apart and prayed again, as we still plodded on. Again came the answer, 'Turn to the left, to the Godavari, and you will find rescue.'

"Again I called to the guides and questioned them: 'Are you sure there is no rising ground by the river where we can pitch, with the river on one side for protection and campfires around us on the other, through the night?'

" 'None whatever.'

" 'Think well; is there no dry timber of which we could make a raft?'

" 'If there were any, it would all be washed away by these floods.'

" 'Is there no boat of any sort on the river? I have authority to seize anything I need.'

" 'None nearer than the cataract.'

" 'How long would it take us to reach the Godavari by the nearest path?'

" 'Half an hour; but it would be so much time lost, for we would have to come back here again, and cut our way through this jungle to the bluff, and climb that; there is no other way of getting around these two flooded streams that we must pass to reach the cataract.'

" 'How long would it take us to cut our way through to the bluff?'

" 'At least six hours; it will be dark in an hour.'

" 'What shall we do for tonight?'

" 'God knows.' And they looked the despair they felt.

"I drew aside again and prayed as I rode on. 'Turn to the left, to the Godavari, and you will find rescue,' came the response the third time. It was not audible; none of those near heard it. I cannot explain it, but to me it was as distinct as though spoken by a voice in my ear; it thrilled me. 'God's answer to my prayer,' said I, 'I cannot doubt. I must act, and that instantly.'

"Hastening forward to the guides at the head of the column, 'Halt!' said I, in a voice to be heard by all. 'Turn sharp to the left. Guides, show us the shortest way to the Godavari. Quick!'

"They remonstrated stoutly that it was only labor lost, that we should be in a worse plight there than here, for the river might rise higher and wash us away in the darkness of the night.

" 'Obey!' said I. 'March sharp, or night will come. I am master here, and intend to be obeyed. Show the way to the river.'

"All the party had surrounded me. My native preacher looked up inquiringly at my awed face. 'There is rescue at the river,' was all I said. How could I say more?"

Driving his guides before him by sheer dominating will, the missionary soon broke through to the Godavari bank. And, lo, there he saw the way of refuge! At that very moment an excited boat crew were struggling to tie up a big barge to a tree on the bank. The barge had broken loose, far above, and at no place could they stop it till just at this moment. Here was safety for the night and transport for the morrow. The boatmen were fearful, thinking Doctor Chamberlain an official. "Please don't be angry with us. We did our best to keep the boat from coming here; but, sir, it seemed as though it was 'possessed.' " The missionary knew well the Hand that had interposed.

In the World War

Young L——, who had his nurses' training at one of our sanitariums in Germany, was assigned to the sanitary and hospital department during the World War. Of one experience he told me:

"We were under fire on the field. The air was humming with missiles, and shells were falling all about. So hot was the rain of fire that our company took refuge in an underground dugout.

"We were all safely down the passage, crowded together in the dark shelter, when a voice cried to me, 'Go out!'

" 'No,' I said, thinking my reply to the message. 'There's safety here, and it's dangerous out there.'

"But like a trumpet call in my soul was that ringing command, 'Go out!'

"I felt that it was from God, and that I could not resist it.

"Immediately I jumped up and ran up the passage and into the open again. The shower of death was still falling, but I sat down on the ground in a hollow place, though altogether unsheltered. The next instant, it seemed, a high-powered heavy shell fell upon the dugout, piercing it and digging a great crater!"

Yet another story of a voice that called to safety was told me by Evangelist F——, who gave me this text as one that had been precious to him: "He that is our God is the God of salvation; and unto God the Lord belong the issues from death." Ps. 68:20.

"On the 12th of September, 1916," he said, "I was taking shelter in a shell hole, one of those deep craters dug out by an exploding bomb. There was a company of others in the same crater, and we were under severe fire. Suddenly a voice spoke to me. It was spoken to my heart or mind, and not audibly, but it was just as plain as if the command had come to my ears: 'Quick! Out of here!'

"At once I told the others who were there that I was impressed that we should leave that place immediately. Five men followed me as I sprang out. The next instant a high-

5

powered shell fell into the very place where we had been! The voice of warning had saved our lives.

"My comrades wept for joy as they saw it, thankful that I had been with them to warn them. They understood that I feared God, and that it was He who had delivered us."

Called Into the Light

In a Minnesota city a Roman Catholic lady secured a Bible. She was concerned for her soul. When she talked with her priest, he was so unsympathetic and abrupt that she lost confidence in him. As she prayed for help, a voice said to her: "Leave the Catholic Church!"

She felt the call was from God, and began to attend Protestant religious meetings. She had visited fourteen places, when one night, still searching for the right way, she and her husband came to a Seventh-day Adventist service conducted by Evangelist D. F. Weatherly. The evangelist told me the sequel:

"She showed such interest that I invited her to come to our Sabbath meetings at the church, explaining that Saturday was the day.

"The lady laughed and said, 'You mean Sunday.'

" 'No, Saturday. That is the Sabbath.'

" 'But will there be any one there?' asked the lady.

" 'Yes.'

"So the lady came. She was deeply impressed with the service and the worship.

" 'May I attend here?' she asked, after the meeting.

" 'Yes, surely,' I replied, and since then she has been baptized into the faith."

The Arresting Voice

In beautiful Jamaica, in the West Indies, a woman had persistently refused to heed the lesson of the Bible studies one of our gospel workers had held with her. "No," she declared, "I shall always go to market on Saturdays!" Then suddenly came a change. The worker relates the experience:

"One Saturday, she said, while she was coming from the

market with her load on her head, as she was just about to take the branch road that leads to her home, she was suddenly stopped and remained at the spot for about a quarter of an hour in great physical agony; and she distinctly heard a voice saying, 'Why do you go to the market today? Don't you know that today is the Sabbath of the Lord thy God? In it no man shall do any work; for whosoever knoweth the Master's will and doeth it not, shall be beaten with many stripes. Now will you kneel down and pray?'

"She said she was somewhat timid, and hesitated to kneel down in the middle of the road, it being a market day; but as her great agony immediately left her, she moved to one side and offered a sincere prayer. From that moment she surrendered to follow the Lord fully."

The Voice That Said, "Go Back!"

It was in Oregon that Colporteur B——, with a book on Bible topics, had bidden good day to a Mrs. M——. As he showed the book, a friend of hers had come in and advised her against the book. But as he passed out, the servant maid said to him, "I am sure Mrs. M—— wants that book." The sale was clearly lost—and yet not lost. The sequel, as told me in Oregon, follows:

"The colporteur went on his way, taking an order at the next house, and meeting a former customer who had followed him to order a second copy for his son.

"Rejoicing over putting out the good books, but regretting the failure to get an order from the lady where he had first called, he turned into the main road to pass on.

"Then there came to him in what seemed an audible voice, 'Go back and sell Mrs. M—— a book!' He looked about, almost startled, the words were so clear; but he could see no one. 'I thought,' he said, 'that some boys over the hedge must have heard of my failure to sell the book, and were making sport of it, as boys sometimes will.' He drove on a hundred yards, and then a second time he heard the same voice; and as the brother marveled at it, a third time the words came

more commandingly clear, 'I say, go back and sell Mrs. M——
a book.' This time the horse almost stopped still. 'I felt
now that it was truly of the Lord,' said the colporteur. 'I
said, "Yes, Lord, I will go." I was scarcely conscious of
turning the horse around, but he whirled about, and we were
off to return to the first house.'

"Arrived at the place, the colporteur found Mrs. M——
out in the garden. 'I beg pardon, Mrs. M——,' he began without preliminaries, 'but I know you want the book, and I have
called to see which binding I shall order for you.'

" 'I have always been partial to the leather binding,' she
replied, 'and you may order that for me.' "

The book proved a blessing indeed in that home, bringing
to the lady a new experience in Christ. And in the divine
plan of Providence, evidently, just then was the time for her
to get that new experience; for very shortly afterward she
died in the full assurance of hope.

"Take the Other Road"

In pioneering days in Brazil one of our evangelists was
holding meetings in a remote settlement, where many Catholics were being interested in Bible truth. Bitter opposition
arose, and a group of men laid plans to beat up the preacher
the next time he came, Director F. W. Spies reported:

"A secret plan was laid, and some thirty of the enemies of
the truth gathered at a small rumshop by the road where the
worker was expected to pass. They then encouraged each
other by drinking more rum and telling how they would flog
the preacher. They even tied the gate through which he must
pass, and felt sure they had him in their power.

"The worker, however, was entirely ignorant of this plot,
and was planning on taking this, the usual road, as he jour-
neyed on the following day. There was another road, which
would take the worker to the same destination, but it was more
difficult and less traveled.

"On the morning of his departure, as he was saddling his
mule to continue his journey, the conviction seized him, and

it seemed almost like an audible voice, saying to him, 'Take the other road.' Though the old and known road would have been far preferable, he obeyed what seemed to him the Lord's guidance, though he could not then understand it, and was soon well on his way.

"Not small was his surprise when, upon a later visit, the worker was informed of the plan of the opposers, and he realized how marvelously the Lord had led him and frustrated the designs of the would-be persecutors of His servant."

Warned to Escape

Soon after the opening of Rhodesia (South Africa) to settlement, our old Solusi Mission was established among the Matabeles, just over twenty miles from Bulawayo. In 1896 came the Matabele rebellion. The missionaries had to gather for safety in Bulawayo. But as the war was prolonged, members of the staff now and then made journeys by night to the station to secure food supplies. In his book, "On the Trail of Livingstone," W. H. Anderson tells of a spoken warning that saved his life one night. He had been at the station, and then made a visit to the kraal of a friendly chief, Solusi, four miles away. He says:

"On my way back, a voice spoke to me, saying, 'Get out of here quickly, for you are in danger!'

"I wondered where the danger could come from, but hurried along the path as fast as I could run. That night I feared to sleep in our house at the mission, so took my blankets and slept in the thick bush about half a mile away.

"Next morning some friendly natives came up to the house, and asked what path I had taken on the way home from Solusi's kraal the night before. I told them which path I had taken, and they asked me where I was when the sun went down. I told them I was near the river.

"They looked at one another in astonishment, and inquired if I had seen none of the rebels. I said, 'No.' Then I learned that within a few minutes after I heard the warning voice, about 300 of the rebels came down another footpath into the one along which I was traveling, and went on to Solusi's kraal.

"Again I was reminded of the assurance, 'The angel of the Lord encampeth round about them that fear Him, and delivereth them.' "

Led to the Word by Night

Brought into touch with mission work in one of our great Eastern cities, a lady whose father was a Jew and her mother a Catholic, told me how God had directly called her to seek the light of truth. She said:

"I had known nothing of the Bible. At the time of which I speak, my husband had been called away on business, and I was alone for the night in my home.

"Soon after midnight I awoke, startled. Somehow a terrible fear was upon me. I could not explain it, but it was so real that I feared to stay in the house alone. A voice, calling me by name, said, 'Go to the hotel and take a room.' I got up about one o'clock in the morning. When I was shown to the room at the hotel, I saw a book lying on the table in my room. It was one of the Bibles which the Gideon League distributes among hotels throughout the country. It was a new book to me.

"Thoroughly awake, I sat up the rest of the night and read that Bible. By early morning I wanted a Bible of my own. At first I thought I would ring for the boy, and tell him to ask the manager if I might not buy that copy. Then I thought it would appear strange, and they would think I was not quite balanced, coming to the hotel at one o'clock in the morning, and then early in the morning trying to buy a Bible from them. So I went home.

"A friend called. I said, 'Have you a Bible?' 'Surely,' she said, 'I have two or three of them.' 'Let me have one,' I said. So, finding myself in possession of a Bible, I began to study it."

Very soon the lady was rejoicing in the experience of personal faith in Christ and His salvation. In telling me the story, the narrator said she could never cease to thank God that He woke her up that night so strangely, and sent her to the hotel to come in touch with His holy word.

To the Japanese Inquirer

Evangelist Kuniya, of Japan, reported many years ago:

"An old lady about sixty years of age became interested and attended our meetings regularly. However, her husband and son opposed her, and she finally stopped coming.

"A few days ago she called one of our young workers, and related her experience. 'For some time,' she said, 'I was troubled greatly because my family opposed my attending your meetings. I thought it not good to disturb the peace of the home with my new religion, so decided to study and pray alone; but one night I was shown that I should attend the meetings.

" 'I heard a voice say, "If you stop going to church, your soul will die." Still I had not the courage to go. Very soon I was taken sick, and suffered for several days. I prayed the Lord to heal me, but the answer was, "No." I was perplexed and disappointed; but last night I saw the sin of neglecting to heed the warning of the messenger, and repented, and prayed to the Lord to heal me. Now the fever has left me, and I have promised to attend the meetings, and also to tell my friends and relatives of this truth.' "

She accepted Christ, and her testimony was a blessing to others.

┌──┐
HELPED INTO LIGHT BY A DREAM

"In a dream . . . He openeth the ears of men, and sealeth their instruction." Job 33:15, 16.
└──┘

Faith Rests Upon the Written Word

IT is not that faith rests upon any impressions, merely. "Faith cometh by hearing, and hearing by the word of God." Rom. 10:17. But from earliest times God has used every means to prepare hearts to receive His word. He spoke by dream to the pagan Abimelech, king of Gerar, in Abraham's day, and used Balaam, a man untrue to Him, to speak messages to the heathen Balak. As the author of "Lead, Kindly Light" wrote:

> "Mid Balak's magic fires
> The Spirit spake, clear as in Israel;
> With prayers untrue and covetous desires
>   Did God vouchsafe to dwell;
> Who summoned dreams, His earlier word to bring
> To patient Job's vexed friends, and Gerar's guileless king. . . .
> Why should we fear the Son now lacks His place
>   Where roams unchristened man?
> As though, where faith is keen, He cannot make
> Bread of the very stones, or thirst with ashes slake."

In regions where the Bible is not so accessible it seems that Providence more frequently works by means out of the ordinary, to awaken inquiry and prepare men and women to receive help from those who have light. No one should pay attention to the mere pointless dreams of troubled sleep; but when these things are used to awaken souls to search for light and bring forth definite fruits of obedience, we may recognize the intervening hand of God.

In Remote Ethiopia

One of our pioneer missionaries of Abyssinia, G. Gudmundsen, has briefly told the story of a man strangely called and clearly used. In quoting I abbreviate:

70

"More than half of our membership in Ethiopia is from Begember, where years ago lived Sheik Zacharias. He was born of a wealthy Mohammedan family. He sought in the Koran for peace in his soul. It is said he knew the whole Koran from memory. He found no peace. Then a dream came to him one night. It was as though an angel stood by his side with a book. Zacharias saw it was the Bible. 'Read this book,' said the angel, 'and you will find peace for your soul.' A little later he came into possession of a Bible. The more he read, the more clearly he realized that truth was found in the Bible alone. . . .

"He gathered a few of his most trusted friends, read the Bible to them, and finally convinced them of its truth. The number of disciples soon were reckoned by hundreds, then thousands. Zacharias met strong opposition from the Mohammedans, and also from the Christian Coptic priests. Opponents were unable to resist his presentations, as he was so close a student of both Bible and Koran. He appeared before the Emperor Menelik, who was so impressed as to grant religious freedom to the sheik and his followers. These had continual trouble because of refusal to adore the pictures of the saints. They said, 'We know only one God, the Creator of the heavens and the earth, and know only one Saviour, Jesus Christ. We cannot bow ourselves before others.'

"Before his death, Zacharias instructed his followers: 'Someday greater light will come to you in Bible truth.' He told them of a dream he had one night. He saw in the dream a great light that spread over Ethiopia. A voice said to him: 'There will come messengers to you with greater light, and when these come, you must accept them.' 'Now,' said Zacharias, 'when these new messengers come, then the message which I, Zacharias, have brought you, will be as the light of the moon compared to the light of the midday sun.' He admonished them to hold fast until the new light should come."

Years after the death of Zacharias, some of his people, visiting our first mission in Eritrea, found the message they were waiting for. The two visitors were instructed and baptized. It was the first fruits of our work for these people, among whom we have had encouraging success.

"You Must Buy That Book"

In South America, says N. P. Neilsen, many have had their attention first drawn to our books by dreams. Here is one case:

"A colporteur presented his book to a certain man. The man did not want it, was not interested. While the colporteur stood there, the man's wife came in. Like Pilate's wife, who came in with the message of a dream warning the Roman proconsul not to condemn Jesus, this wife came hurrying in to her husband. 'You must buy that book,' she said; 'for I had a dream last night. I haven't told you. But in a dream I saw a man come with this hand satchel that the gentleman has, and with this very book that he brings with him. Buy it.' The colporteur eventually left eight people keeping the Sabbath in that place."

Directed to the Right Place

In the earlier years of our evangelistic work in north England, Evangelist A. S. Rodd related to me this story of a woman who had been praying for a clearer view of truth:

"One night in a dream, she told us, it seemed to her that an angel came and spoke to her. In the dream she said to the angel:

" 'I do not see how you can find the time to come to me.'

"Her visitant replied: 'I can spare time always to visit any one who wants the truth.'

"He beckoned her to follow, and led her to a mission hall, and pointing her to a certain seat in the hall, he bade her listen here and receive the truth. 'You will find the truth here,' the angel said. Then she awoke.

" 'Ever since,' she said to us, 'I have looked for that mission hall.'

"She had searched long up and down the city, visiting one place and then another, without finding the hall of which she had so vivid an impression.

" 'But here I see it tonight,' she said, 'and there,' pointing to a certain chair, 'is the very place where I sat in my dream.'

"Needless to say, she was an attentive listener as the meetings continued, and with joy she accepted fully the message for these times."

If all the angels are "ministering spirits, sent forth to minister for them who shall be heirs of salvation," why should it be considered incredible that an angel should visit a praying soul and point the way to the place of truth? One cheering lesson of the story is the evidence it gives that God knows every home in all the great cities where a soul is praying for light.

The Burmese Dentist Prepared

A Buddhist dentist, dissatisfied with his religion, had this experience, as told me by Evangelist Chit Hla in Burma:

"He saw two men coming to his house, dressed all in white, which was an unusual garb there, so that he remembered it. Then it was said to him: 'These men will tell you of the Lord of peace.' In the dream he asked which was the true church, Catholic or Baptist? The answer was, 'The true church will tell you about the prophecy. A King is soon coming, who will rule the whole world. These men will reveal to you about that coming King.' "

Two or three months later our evangelist Chit Hla and his helper, Maung Potok, called at the dentist's house. That day they were clad all in white. The evangelist told how the dentist came at once to the point:

" 'Tell me about the World Ruler who is to come.'

"I opened my Bible to Daniel 2, and gave an explanation of that prophecy. When I finished, he said, 'You are the men I saw in a dream.' Then he related to us the experience that had prepared him for our call. He accepted the truth with joy."

Chart of the Sanctuary Service a Guide

In China a Buddhist girl had ventured, on invitation of Mrs. Bothilde Miller, to attend a special Bible study institute.

Timid and fearful under the strange surroundings and teaching, she was ill at ease, until the evangelist hung up a chart illustrating the service in the two apartments of the earthly sanctuary, as a type of Christ's ministry for us in the heavenly sanctuary. Then the Buddhist girl was all attention. Conviction came to her heart. She explained later:

"Three months ago I had a dream in which I saw the view that now I have seen represented on the chart. I saw the high priest in the service, and everything as pictured on the chart. Now I know this is the truth. I am so glad I have found this truth."

Waiting in Iceland

Visiting remote Sagas Island, off the coast of Iceland, O. J. Olsen wrote:

"A young colporteur came to a farm cottage and found an elderly man sitting in his chair, as if waiting for him. As our worker entered, the man stood and said, 'Then you are coming.' The colporteur did not understand. The man said: 'I think the Lord has let me know of you before this. Last night, while I was sleeping, some one called my name and said, "Tomorrow you will have a chance to see things you long to see. A man will come to you with books and a paper." I heard the name of the paper.' As our colporteur showed our Icelandic paper, the man said, 'That is it.' It is not to be wondered at that the man bought books and papers and gave himself to the study of the truth."

"Come In; This Is God's Truth"

Evangelist J. M. Howell, when in the Chile Conference, South America, found a man in a remote part who had been obeying the truth for nineteen years. "How did you learn of this way?" he asked. The man answered:

"Twenty years ago there were some Protestants who came to this neighborhood and began work. Although I knew nothing about them, I opposed them. But one night I had a dream. In the dream I was walking through the streets of the town, and I heard some people singing. It was very pretty, and as we came along beside the house in which they were singing, I saw a man standing at the door who said, 'Come in; this is God's truth.' As I stepped in, I saw a man standing before an audience, talking to them.

"The next day I went to see one of my cousins. She said, 'I have become interested in some Protestant meetings. Wouldn't you like to go with me tonight to the church?' Remembering my dream, I said, 'Yes,' and so that evening we started down town. As we drew near the place, I heard singing that sounded very much like what I had heard in my dream, and as we came to the door, a man said, 'Come in; this is God's truth.' We stepped in, and I saw the very same man that I had seen in my dream the night before, who was just getting up to talk to the people. I was really impressed by the voice of God calling me to follow Him, and these nineteen years I have been trying to be faithful to Him as best I could."

A Colporteur's Dream

Colporteur E. Sanchey, in Mexico, told this story:

"One night while on a tour I had a dream that a man would take a Bible and say to me, 'Sir, take the Bible and speak to me from the word of God.' I awoke and wished that it were day already, so that I might be on my way. That day I visited a gentleman whose name had been given me by the mayor of the town. The gentleman showed me his library, and said he had a very fine book to show me. He picked up a Bible, and said, 'Take this Bible and teach me the word of God, and tell me about the seventh-day Sabbath, because I know you people sanctify that day by order of God.' Then I remembered my dream, and about the man who was represented as coming to me and saying, 'Sir, take the Bible and teach me from the word of God.' When I finished talking with him, he assured me that he wanted to become a faithful Adventist. He invited others to join him in his decision, and as a result, a large group are anxiously waiting for a worker to arrive and give them studies."

Way Prepared Five Years in Advance

Here is a story of preparation of the way in the Philippines, told by R. R. Figuhr, superintendent of the Philippine Union Mission. He says:

"Some of our brethren were doing Harvest Ingathering work for missions in the province of Neuva Ecija. One came to a home where the man asked what we believe. He was told that we believe in the soon coming of Christ and the seventh-day Sabbath. A smile came over the man's face, for he remembered that five years before he had seen in a dream an angel standing before him, preaching to him from a book. The angel told him of the coming of the Lord and of His true Sabbath, and also told him that a man would come to tell him all things, but that he would have to wait five years for this man to come. 'Now,' the man said, 'you have come, and as this is five years after, you must be the people whom the angel foretold. Where is your church? I want to attend.'

"The brethren told him of our church in the city, and he has joined the Sabbath school and is preparing for baptism."

If these recitals, becoming now so common, were only interesting stories, it would hardly pay to put them into print. They are more than interesting; they show that God is pouring out His Spirit far ahead of us, and that angels are all abroad in the world.

Directed to the Street Number

The leader of the book work in the southern part of South America, J. L. Brown, has made public the following report of a colporteur in Chile:

"I did not know just where to start my work in the city; therefore I earnestly prayed that the Lord would lead me. That night I dreamed dreams. I was shown in my dream that I should begin my work with number 687 on —— street.

"The following morning I set out to find the street I had seen in my dream. I finally arrived at number 687, but it was only a garage. I walked past the place several times, wondering why I should enter there and begin my work, since it was just a garage. But in my prayer I had asked the Lord to lead me, and in my dream I was shown this street and number; so I decided to enter and talk with the manager.

"After I had given the gentleman a canvass, he ordered a copy of the book, and then gave me permission to work among the other men in the garage. As a result my list was nicely started with seven orders taken from the employees of this garage."

As Colporteurs Go From House to House

New York State.—"I met a man Monday morning who told me he had had a dream in which he saw one bringing him the very book I had."

Brazil.—"A woman told me she had a dream in which she saw a dark world, but in the midst of a field of light she saw a people, each one with a book, which proved to be the Bible. The husband said: 'Now we want that book, and also wish to join the people in the light.' They and a number of other near-by families are keeping the Sabbath."

Hungary.—"I know what you have to show me," said a lady to the colporteur at her door. "You have a book in your brief case. I saw you and the brief case and the book in a dream only last night."

Western Canada.—"In a dream I saw you come with this book, and I want it," said a farmer to a colporteur. "But in the dream you had also a little black book in which you wrote. What is that?" "That is this little book," said the colporteur, taking out the black-covered book of guaranty slips. "I sign one of these blanks and give it to you as a guaranty that the book will be like the copy I have shown you."

"That Very Book."—"I called last Friday at the home of a woman who had been in an automobile wreck. She had just returned home from the hospital. The doctors said there was no hope for her and that she must die. Shortly after this she felt impressed to go home. She told the doctors that she must go home, and she had been there just about an hour when I called upon her. She said, 'I saw you and that very book in

my dream last night.' Then she said, 'I have great faith in God, and believe He can heal me. I want you to kneel here and lay your hand on my head and pray for me.' After I had prayed earnestly, she arose, said she was healed, and declared, 'God sent you here.' "

So from east and west, and from far north to far south, all the time come the reports that show how Providence prepares the way for souls to give attention to the light. The prophecy of the closing gospel work is fulfilling:

"It shall come to pass afterward, that I will pour out My Spirit upon all flesh; . . . your old men shall dream dreams, your young men shall see visions." Joel 2:28.

"Turned to flight the armies of the aliens." Heb. 11:34.

In the olden times of the Bible story, again and again the invisible armies of heaven sent the spirit of fear and flight into hosts arrayed against the people of God. When the days came for the cutting short of the persecuting power of the Papacy, the Lord surely wrought "as in the ancient days."

The Papal Forces Fled in Terror

To suppress the cause of the Bohemian reformed party, Pope Martin, in 1427, had encouraged a real crusade to crush Ziska and his slender forces. Electors, princes, counts, and a special papal legate led the host. Wylie tells how at last the papal army caught up with the Bohemians:

"The two armies were separated only by the river that flows past Meiss. The crusaders were in greatly superior force, but instead of dashing across the stream, and closing in battle with the Hussites whom they had come so far to meet, they stood gazing in silence. . . . It was only for a few moments that the invaders contemplated the Hussite ranks. A sudden panic fell upon them. They turned and fled in the utmost confusion. The legate was as one who awakens from a dream. His labors and hopes at the very moment when, as he thought, they were to be crowned with victory, suddenly vanished in a shameful rout."—*"The History of Protestantism," book 3, chap. 17.*

A yet greater force was sent against the Bohemians in 1431. At last the armies faced each other. Cardinal Cesarini, the pope's special representative, climbed a hill to see the triumph, as the knights in arms and the helmeted cavalry went forth to conquest. And what did he see? Let Wylie tell it:

"The cardinal and his friend had gazed only a few minutes when they were startled by a strange and sudden movement in the host. As if smitten by some invisible power, it appeared all at once to break up and scatter. The soldiers threw away their armor and fled, one this way, another that; and the wagoners, emptying their vehicles of their load, set off across the plain at full gallop.

"Struck with consternation and amazement, the cardinal hurried down to the field, and soon learned the cause of the catastrophe. The army had been seized with a mysterious panic. That panic extended to the officers equally with the soldiers. The Duke of Bavaria was one of the first to flee. He left behind him his carriage, in the hope that its spoil might tempt the enemy and delay their pursuit. Behind him, also in inglorious flight, came the Elector of Brandenburg; and following close on the elector were others of less note, chased from the field by this unseen terror. The army followed, if that could be styled an army which so lately had been a marshaled and bannered host, but was now only a rabble rout, fleeing when no man pursued."

History gives no natural explanation. As Wylie adds: "There is here the touch of a divine finger—the infusion of a preternatural terror."

How Providence Intervened Among the Nations

Many a story might be recited of special deliverances in behalf of believers and leaders in the time of the Reformation of the sixteenth century that broke the universal power of the Papacy and began to cut short the days of persecution. But the deliverance of the cause of the Reformation itself is a record of the continuous working of the intervening hand. God caused "the wrath of man" to "praise Him" (Ps. 76:10), moving great nations to and fro and holding opposing powers in check, in order that the Reformation might not be crushed.

Let a secular history (Johnson's "Europe in the Sixteenth Century") outline the story of the providential overruling of wars and political rivalries to divert the attention of rulers who otherwise would have oppressed believers:

The Year 1521.—The Diet of Worms had condemned

Luther, and the emperor Charles V expected to enforce the decree. But—

"At this moment the attention of Charles was directed to the war against Francis [king of France]. The humiliation of his rival and the conquest of Italy were the first essentials; till these were attained, the affair of Luther might wait."

And all the time Luther and his associates were teaching and publishing and the leaven of reform was spreading.

1524.—The emperor now fiercely denounced Luther. The Congress of Ratisbon forbade the reading of his books. If pope and emperor had acted in concert, says this history, something might have been done to crush the young cause. We read:

"But this was prevented by the political issues, which once more drove them apart, and so monopolized Charles's attention that, as he said, 'This was no time to speak of Luther.'"

1525.—Charles had won out over Francis at Pavia. The uprising of the peasants in Germany, stirred up by the fanatical Münzer, a professed Reformer, had brought great reproach upon the cause of true reform. Now Charles was convinced that "heresy and rebellion" were the same. Now he would "crush out heresy" with no more delay. Then suddenly came trouble in Italy that led to his campaign that ended in the sack of Rome itself. The history says:

"In the midst of the troubles of the Italian campaign, and in the face of the hostility of the pope, any decisive action against the Reformers had been out of the question. It was at least necessary to procrastinate."

1530-32.—All the time the cause of reform was growing. In 1529 the princes had presented the famous Protest at Spires, that gave us the name of Protestants. No longer could the emperor let matters go. At the Diet of Augsburg he gave the Protestants till April, 1531, to come into line. After that date "measures were to be taken for the extirpation of their sect." But ere that date, trouble was upon the emperor in floods. The Turks under Solyman I were threatening to invade the empire. As head of the Holy Roman

Empire, it was the duty of Charles to put down heresy, but "his position as king of Germany forced him to postpone the suppression of heresy to the imperative necessity of gaining the support of the Protestants against the Turk."

1539.—By this time most of the strongest princes of Germany were with the party of reform. "The crisis demanded instant action." But now Francis of France broke out again. "With the prospect of war before him, the emperor recognized the impossibility of using force against the Protestants."

1544.—By the treaty with France, says the history, "the hands of the emperor were at last free to deal with the Protestants in Germany."

But now he had waited so long that the suppression of the cause of reform was beyond the reach of the sword. Whole principalities and countries had espoused the cause. Those who had the intent to strike down the cause of the Reformation were prevented continually. Nations and peoples were in surging waves of convulsion, like stormy waves of the sea clashing against one another. In the midst of political controversies, the friends of the Reformation escaped attention and did their work. They could say with the psalmist: "If it had not been Jehovah who was on our side, when men rose up against us; then they had swallowed us up alive." These things surely have a lesson for our day. Amid political contests and the clashing of great forces, the cause of truth, under the protecting hand of Providence, is to make its way to final victory.

ATTACKERS RESTRAINED

"No weapon that is formed against thee shall prosper."
Isa. 54:17.

NOT always is it to God's glory that violence is restrained. We cannot interpret the providence that sustains one in suffering death and another in deliverance from the peril. But the promise has ever held true, "My grace is sufficient for thee." Again and again the arm lifted to strike has been held powerless.

Could Not Draw the Knife

At a meeting on Cebu, one of the southern islands of the Philippines, evangelists were telling experiences. One said:

"A man said he would kill me. He tried to draw his knife from the sheath, but could not get it out. He struck me in the face with his hand. I did not retaliate. He tried again to draw the knife. Ten times he tried, and failed. So he struck me again with his hand. Then shame came over him. He said he felt that a power supernatural had held him from drawing the knife. He begged my forgiveness. Since then, the brethren report, he seems to have become seriously interested in the message."

Then another told this story:

"One day a man came to me holding out his bolo [the large swordlike knife used in field work]. 'Here it is,' he said; 'it is the knife with which I intended to kill you when you began to hold these meetings. I am different now. I want you to forgive me.' "

And the evangelist added that later this man gave his heart to God and was baptized.

The Hired Attacker

One of our leaders in South America, Evangelist Pedro Brouchy, told of an evangelist who encountered fierce opposition in one part of the Argentine. Enemies hired a notorious gangster to put an end to the preaching. Armed with a long knife, the assassin came to the meeting. The preacher began to speak.

"Soon," we are told, "the man with his wicked knife concealed began to feel something strange taking place in his mind and heart. The operation of the 'two-edged sword' was going on, but he did not understand it."

This first time the evil man was not ready to strike. He went a second time to do the murder. But the account continues:

"Again the 'two-edged sword,' the word of God, overpowered him, and at last he decided to surrender his all to the Master. That night he returned to the group of men who had hired him, and told them that from now on he would attend all the meetings to protect the evangelist, and 'woe unto the man who attempts to do him any harm.'

"Some time later this would-be assassin confessed all his evil intentions in first coming to the meetings. He could not restrain his emotions as he told the story of how the 'two-edged sword' had clashed with his wicked knife, and had won the victory. He was baptized and is now a humble child of God."

Officers Powerless to Give the Order to Fire

During troublous times in Bolivia, when there had been disorder at home and war on the border, Missionary Replogle led a large company of Indian believers from his mission school to a place of baptism on the pampa (plain). He noticed a company of soldiers gathering not far away, but supposed they were out for training. Later, however, he was ordered into the city of La Paz for investigation. The South American Division *Bulletin* tells the story:

"On the way to the capital, his custodian, a civil officer called a subprefecto, remarked to Brother Replogle: 'I do not understand why you were not killed yesterday.' Upon being questioned, he explained the significance of the movement of troops which Brother Replogle had witnessed and innocently misunderstood the previous day. They had been sent there to anticipate any further trouble among the Indians, and with ruthless hand to put it down. The two or three hundred Indians marching across the pampa appeared as thousands to the excited imagination of the soldiery. Immediately bombing planes were requested from the capital, and the encounter with the hostile(!) Indians awaited. The company was given orders to exterminate the whole company of Indians, but the captain, feeling restrained from giving the order to fire, called upon the sergeant to do so. This noncommissioned officer was equally powerless to pronounce the fatal word. While they were hesitating, or really, while they were being restrained 'supernaturally,' as the subprefecto expressed it, it was seen that what appeared to be an uprising was a baptism of Evangelistas (as non-Catholic Christians are called). Upon arriving in La Paz, Evangelist Replogle and his companion, after reporting at police headquarters, were allowed to go. Thus the Lord sent His angel to protect the lives of His servants in these times of war and trouble as He did in times of old."

Accusing Lips Sealed

In 1542 an edict of death was issued against Menno Simons, leader of Baptist believers in Europe. A reward was offered in Holland for his apprehension. His daughter told the following story of deliverance:

"A man agreed with the magistrates to deliver my father up for a sum of money, or lose his head. One day he went with an officer to arrest him. Menno passed by in a boat, but the man said nothing until he saw Menno land some distance off, and then he exclaimed, 'See! the bird is flown.' The officer called him a villain. 'Why did you not speak before?' He answered, 'I could not speak; for my tongue was held.' The would-be informer lost his head. The sleuth-hound persecutors of Menno Simons missed their prey. He died a natural death at the age of sixty-five."

The same God who sent His angel to shut the mouths of

lions in Daniel's day, must have sent His angels to shut the lips of this would-be informer.

In the Days of the Methodist Revival

John Nelson, a stonecutter Methodist preacher, met a furious mob at Horbury, England. They boasted they would put a rope round his neck and drag him into the river. Hurst says:

"The parson's son, as captain of the mob, had six large hand bells brought from the clerk's house, and these were rung violently that his voice might not be heard. A half-crazed man, six feet tall, was to put the halter round his neck, and a butcher held the rope. Nelson only pushed the halter from his neck, and the man fell as if he had been knocked down with an ax; the butcher stood trembling, and touched him not.

"A shout was raised as the constable approached to arrest him, and the bells were silenced. Without hesitating a moment, Nelson said, 'I am glad you are come, and I charge you in the king's name to do your office.' He asked, 'What is my office?' Nelson answered firmly, 'It is to quell this mob, and deliver me out of their hands.' The constable turned pale, finally bade the mob be silent, and said to Nelson, 'Follow me.' He went to the stable, led out the horse and held the stirrup, led Nelson through the crowd, and bade him go in the name of the Lord!"—*"History of Methodism," Vol. I, p. 491.*

Uplifted Arms Fell Helpless

John Wesley, at Falmouth, was beset by a mob in 1746. He wrote afterward:

"I never saw before, no, not even at Walsall, the hand of God so clearly shown as here. There I received some blows, was covered with dirt, and lost part of my clothes. Here, although the hands of hundreds of people were lifted up to strike or throw, yet they were one and all stopped in the midway; so that not a man touched me with his fingers; neither was anything thrown from first to last; so that I had not a speck of dirt upon my clothes. Who can deny that God heareth prayer? or that He hath all power in heaven and earth?"—*"Wesley's Works," Vol. VII, p. 357.*

Charles Wesley said that while preaching at St. Ives, men stopped their ears and rushed at him to pull him down. "But they had no power to touch me," he added. "Several times they lifted up their hands and clubs to strike me," he continued, "but a stronger arm restrained them." He had "an unseen Protector," he said. It was out of such storm and stress of prejudice and intolerance that Charles Wesley wrote the hymn of trust,—

> "Other refuge have I none,
> Hangs my helpless soul on Thee;
> Leave, O leave me not alone!
> Still support and comfort me.
> All my trust on Thee is stayed,
> All my help from Thee I bring;
> Cover my defenseless head
> With the shadow of Thy wing."

When Dr. Adam Clarke Passed Through the Mob

In his great Commentary, writing on Luke 4:30 (where Christ passed "through the midst" of the Nazareth mob), Dr. Clarke told the story of his own deliverance from a mob. The multitude were tearing at the meeting place with crowbar and spade when Adam Clarke opened the door and walked out.

"As soon as the preacher made his appearance, the savages became instantly as silent and as still as night; he walked forward, and they divided to the right and to the left, leaving a passage of about four feet wide, for himself and a young man who followed him, to walk in. He passed on through the whole crowd, not a soul of whom either lifted a hand or spoke one word, till he and his companion had gained the uttermost skirts of the mob. The narrator, who was present on the occasion, goes on to say:

" 'This was one of the most affecting spectacles I ever witnessed: an infuriated mob without any visible cause (for the preacher spoke not one word) became in a moment as calm as lambs. They seemed struck with amazement bordering on stupefaction; they stared and stood speechless; and after they had fallen back to right and left to leave him a free passage, they were as motionless as statues. They assembled with the full purpose to destroy the man who came to show them the way of salvation; but he, passing through the midst of them, went his way. Was not the God of missionaries in this work?' "

In the quietness that followed for a few minutes after the preacher disappeared, the people inside the church also went out and escaped. Then the mob awoke "as from a dream," and broke the windows and otherwise vented their fury on the house."

The One who, passing through the midst of the mob at Nazareth, went His way, has promised the gospel worker, "Lo, I am with you alway, even unto the end of the world."

The Pistol That Failed

These deliverances by restraint of evil intent are not alone in annals of old time or of far lands. Young people, in pursuit of everyday home missionary aims, find the living God a help in time of need. From just over the line in Mexico, L. W. Archbold reports the deliverance of a young Mexican believer. A group of young people were often out giving Bible studies and visiting village people. We are told:

"One Sunday evening on their way home after giving a study, they met some drunken men. They turned to take another street, but two of the men followed them with pistols in their hands. One of the intoxicated men stepped forward and pointed the pistol at one of the sisters. The young lady ran, but the drunken man overtook her and pressed the pistol upon her breast and pulled at the trigger.

"But God protected His own. The man could not move the trigger. They afterward learned the pistol was loaded, but could not go off. The hand of the Lord intervened and delivered our sister from death."

HELP IN COMMON DIFFICULTY AND IN SORE NEED

"Alas, master! for it was borrowed." 2 Kings 6:5.

The Lord Cared

IN common difficulties as well as in sore needs the Bible story bears witness of a God who cares. The young student in Elisha's day had not only lost an axhead, but it was a borrowed tool. He might have worked out the loss somehow, in time; but there was providential help at hand. The prophet Elisha, in faith, caused the iron to swim on the river's surface. "Take it up to thee," he said to the young man. "And he put out his hand, and took it." 2 Kings 6.

The Trial Balance in China

From China, through Treasurer H. W. Christian, of the North China Union, comes the story of a troublesome trial balance in the books of the local Shansi Mission. Chow Hsin Min, the treasurer, reported:

"I had spent two solid days looking for one cent in my trial balance on the mission books. It seemed as if every column had been added correctly, every total entered correctly, but still my trial balance was out one cent. Late on the evening of the second day, while I was still looking for the balance, the thought came to me, 'I have a Friend who can help me find that one cent.' Without further delay, I knelt down and prayed to God that He would help me locate that balance, and that He would show me just where it was.

"After finishing my prayer, I arose to my feet. Then the conviction came to me, 'Look at Mr. ——'s account.' I turned over to that account, and sure enough, there it was—a mistake in addition."

With a note of earnestness he said, "O, how I do appreciate the help of God in my work! Many times I am alone here in the office, and I must make decisions that affect the Lord's work. What else can I do but pray?"

The Needy Seamstress

Because the item concerns a very ordinary trouble I give it here, as a sister told it to me some years ago in Queensland, Australia. In a time when the husband was out of employment, the family needs had to be provided by her needle.

"I had to earn," she said. "I got work on garments, taking the work home. One day I had trouble fitting a collar on a coat. It would not go right. I prayed in my heart by the machine as I struggled; but still it evaded me. I was fairly in despair and discouraged.

"Then I came to my senses. I sat back saying, 'Get thee behind me, Satan.' Then I asked God to come in a special way to my help. I turned back to the machine—and the collar went on just right!

"And that week saw another providence. I needed the week's money badly, but I was prevented on Friday from getting my work ticket to the factory. I would have to wait till the next week. But in the afternoon in came a messenger from the shop with my money. 'How is this?' I asked. The boy said, 'Your ticket was found by the counter, and the manager sent the money.' Strange! I had that ticket in my pocketbook that moment! I never sent it in. And I never knew how he could have found any ticket on which to send me the money. But we needed it badly that day, and I felt that God had truly been my helper."

Aground in the Amazon

Colporteur Andre Gedrath was using a launch on the Lower Amazon, selling books up and down the vast river. He ran fast into a sand bar. Do what he would, he could not budge the launch, and he was far out in the river. Superintendent E. H. Wilcox told the story in the South American Division *Bulletin:*

"His supply of food was gone. Strength failed him to do more than he had done. Some men came traveling up the river in a rowboat. He asked for help, but they told him that the place was too dangerous, and that they could do nothing for him. They also told him that he would have to await the next high tide, which would mean the next full moon. That would require nearly a month.

"Brother Andre was in great distress. He dared not abandon the launch, and he had no food; only God can help a man in such an hour. He prayed, and the same God that heard Daniel of old heard his prayer. He fell asleep, but in the night he was awakened. His launch was floating. Soon he started the engine, and to his great surprise and joy he found himself on his way again.

"It was not long until he caught up with the men in the rowboat who had passed him the day before. They were greatly surprised to see him. They could hardly believe their eyes. They said it was impossible for him to get out of that place. 'It was a miracle that you escaped.' He replied, 'Yes, the God I serve has delivered me.' They then desired to know more about this God. Even as Philip of old preached Christ to the Ethiopian, so did Andre preach Christ to them. They agreed with him that God had delivered, for nothing but an extra high tide could have affected the river there sufficiently to loosen his boat. God, seeing Brother Andre's extreme need, had sent the tide."

The Money by Post

Out of the war-stricken regions of Eastern Europe, in the days following the war, came stories of many a struggle of Protestant believers to keep going in the midst of universal distress, and the hostile feeling against Protestants in some sections. One such family had run out of food. Work had seemed unobtainable. The parents and children were actually in extremity of need. The story was told by L. H. Christian, then president of the European Division:

"The father was praying one morning, with his wife and

children. They were suffering the pangs of starvation, and they turned to God in prayer as their only hope.

"As the father prayed this morning, he seemed to hear a voice saying, 'If you have faith, you will be saved.'

"He took it as assurance of deliverance, and the family thanked God that He had heard their cry.

"Just a little later the mail carrier came to their door with a letter. The letter was opened, and it was found that only money was enclosed. Who it was from they knew not, but there was money for their immediate need. It saved them from threatened starvation, and tided them over until they were able to find ways of earning a livelihood again amid the desolation that the war had left in its wake. I know the facts, for I saw the family only a few weeks ago.

"Some time later the father attended a meeting, held near his home. He there told of his experience, to the glory of God, and added, 'I should like to meet the one who sent me that money.'

"There was a man present who then stood up and said, 'I sent that letter. I sent it before I became an Adventist believer. One night in a dream an envelope, addressed with name and place, was held before me, and a voice commanded, "Put so much money in this envelope, and send it to that man!" I did not know who the man was,' he continued, 'and I never had heard of the place. But it was so clear and commanding an experience that next morning, as I awoke, I felt I must obey. I addressed an envelope as I had seen it in the dream; I put the money in it, and dropped it into the post. After I had done it, it seemed so unreasonable a thing for me to do that I feared I might really be losing my mind. But it was done, and I could not recall it.' "

Soon afterward the man who sent the money was visited by a colporteur, who sold him a book that led him into the light. Hearing of the meeting to be held, he had come to thank God for the light that the open Bible had brought into his life; and there he heard the story of the man to whom he had sent the money, not knowing what he was doing, save that God called him to do it. It was a happy meeting between the two men.

The Bag of Flour

Yet again, from out the war-torn regions of Eastern Europe, comes a story of deliverance in those distressful postwar times. Pastor L. H. Christian, of Europe, once reported:

"A man whom I knew, and his family, were starving. They had not had a bite to eat for two days and a half. Then they saw a miserly man, a man whom they knew never would sell flour unless he received a very high price, hurrying up with his little cart. He pulled out a sack of flour, threw it on his shoulder, and rushed up to the house and set it down, then hastened away as fast as he could. The father rushed out after him and said, 'What do you mean? What about the flour?'

"The man replied, 'I don't know what I mean. I had planned to sell the flour, but have not had any peace for two days. I couldn't sleep at night. I had to come, I don't know why, and put the flour outside your kitchen.'

"So the family thanked God, and were saved."

The Praying Widow

The story just told is similar to one told of the year 1847, known as the "hunger year" in southern Germany. It is recorded by a German writer, Fr. Schwenker, in a little book entitled, "Das Gebet" (Prayer), published years ago in Leipzig. The writer says:

"In the hunger year of 1847, there lived in the neighborhood of Heilbronn a pious man who, one early morning hour, could find no rest. A voice called to him, 'You are to take a bag of meal, and go forth with it. There are many who have nothing to eat, and the Lord will show you what you should do.'

"He placed the bag of meal upon a wheelbarrow, and started forth. He pushed on, however, through the first village, because there seemed no indication that he should turn in at any house. Even so he passed through a second village, and another, until he passed the fourth. Weary, he now came at evening to Heilbronn.

"Suddenly, as he came to a high house, it was said to him, 'There it is!'

"On the first floor and on the second lived well-to-do people. At last, when he reached the top, he said to himself, 'Here it must be,' and he pushed open a door, set the sack of meal inside, saying aloud, 'This the Lord sends to you!' Without waiting, he went on his way.

"In that room as he spoke, a widow was upon her knees, with seven children about her, suffering with hunger almost to the death. And she was praying, 'O Lord, today only have a care for us.' "

Thus over the long road was relief sent to the right place just at the time of need. "Whoso is wise, and will observe these things, even they shall understand the loving-kindness of the Lord." Ps. 107 :43.

"Send Us a Whole Loaf, Lord"

So a little girl prayed in the hunger time of the Russian revolutionary days. Pastor L. H. Christian, of Europe, brought us the story from out of the Baltic Provinces, when he visited there shortly after the war. One of our members, formerly a lady of title, had lost her property in the revolution. Her own children had died, and she had the care of three grandchildren. They struggled for the bare daily bread. The account follows:

"Once the little family were entirely out of food. The little girl was wondering what they would do when the noonday meal had left nothing for the evening lunch. The grandmother assured the children that God would provide some way.

" 'But, grandmother,' the little girl said, 'you don't believe we are going to get anything tonight.'

" 'What makes you think that?' asked the grandmother.

" 'Because you haven't sharpened the knife,' said the little girl.

"They seem to have had a custom in that country by which the housemother at the close of a meal sharpened the bread knife on the edge of the table in token of its use at the next meal; but it seems that somehow the grandmother had failed to sharpen the knife, and the little girl noticed it. So the grandmother sharpened the knife, and together they knelt down to pray God to help them find something more for supper.

"In her prayer the little girl said, 'Lord, don't send us just a piece of bread, send us a whole loaf; for you know, Lord, we need a whole loaf.'

"Through the afternoon they worked at their tasks. Evening came, but no food, and they had no money with which to buy any. It was a severe test of faith to the godly grandmother, who knew that the children were expecting the answer to their prayers.

"But before bedtime that evening there was a knock at the door. As the door was opened, there stood a man, a friend of former prosperous years. He also had been wealthy, but had been despoiled of his property. He had come on foot thirty kilometers (about eighteen and a half miles) through rough weather, to see them.

"As he entered, he said apologetically that he hardly knew why he had come, but that he had been impressed to visit his old friend. Then turning to the children, he said, 'Children, you don't know what I have brought you.'

" 'Yes, we do,' said the little girl.

" 'What have I brought?' the visitor asked.

" 'You have brought us a loaf of bread—not a piece of bread, but a whole loaf,' she answered.

" 'Well, well,' said the visitor, 'how did you know that?'

" 'Because we prayed to God to send us a loaf of bread,' the little girl said, 'and we prayed Him to send us a full, large loaf, for we needed it.'

" 'Well,' said the gentleman, 'that is exactly what I have brought you. That is why I came.'

7

"And out from under his greatcoat which he had worn in the wintry weather, he drew one of those long loaves which the bakers in Europe take from their ovens.

"He had been impressed to come, and surely he came as a messenger sent of God."

THE LESSON OF ELIJAH AND THE RAVENS

"I have commanded the ravens to feed thee there."
1 Kings 17:4.

THROUGH the centuries the story of the raven, bringing food to the prophet Elijah in the days of famine, has encouraged those in need to trust a heavenly Father's care. The Lord has a diversity of resources, as varied as the conditions and needs of men. But there are many experiences on record that remind us of Elijah and the raven.

The Raven in Poland

In his classic history of "English Hymns," Duffield tells of a Polish peasant, named Dobry, a pious Lutheran, who lived near Warsaw, in the time of King Stanislaus (1764-93). The peasant's family were in want, and his landlord was about to turn him from his home in the dead of winter. As he knelt with his wife and children, they sang a hymn of trust as a united prayer to God. Duffield says:

"There was a rap at the window. Dobry went to it, opened it, and a raven which his grandfather had trained and set at liberty popped in with a valuable jeweled ring in its beak. The peasant took the ring at once to his minister, who identified it as the property of King Stanislaus, to whom he restored it.

"The king sent for Dobry, rewarded him handsomely, and the next year built him a new house, and gave him cattle from his own herds. Over this house door, on an iron tablet, appears still, it is said, the effigy of a raven with a ring in its beak."

The prayer that family prayed was Paul Gerhardt's hymn of trust. Our English hymnbook begins it,

"Give to the winds thy fears,
    Hope and be undismayed;
God hears thy sighs and counts thy tears,
    He shall lift up thy head."

The Raven Story in Japan

In a crisis year in Japan, when food was scarce and high, a Christian Japanese found his orphanage family in straits for daily bread. The last small bite was placed before the children for supper. Mr. Ishii told the family the story of Dobry's raven and the ring, and asked the children who would like to do so to go into a little plot at the rear of the home and pray to God for help while he led a prayer season at the church. Nearly thirty of the orphans volunteered, some without tasting the scanty meal before them. The account continues:

"While they were in the act of prayer, there came a call at the door of the orphanage, and a missionary lady, who had that day come to Okayama from another city, entered, bringing thirty-one dollars sent through her to the asylum from a mission band in the State of New York. Mrs. Ishii, to whom she handed the money, seemed dazed, so overwhelmed was she with joy at their unexpected relief from distress, and at the striking coincidence. She sent word immediately to Mr. Ishii, at the church, and a few minutes later the whole story was told in the church prayer meeting."

Actual Ravens in China

In the records of the China Inland Mission is an account by Mrs. Howard Taylor of relief brought an old Christian who was taunted for his faith by a young relative, a priest. The relative often gave the old believer help, for which the man always gave thanks to God. "But why do you thank God for what I do?" said the priest. "It is my heavenly Father who puts it into your heart." "All very well," said the relative; "we shall see." He kept away for a time. The day came when the old believer had not a morsel of food. He conducted a little refuge for opium users who sought freedom. But no one had come in for days, and there was no income. As the old Christian prayed for deliverance, and for a way of testimony to that relative who was testing out his faith, there came a terrible clatter of birds fighting above his roof. He stepped out and saw a flock of ravens being attacked by stronger birds, and in the melee in the air the ravens dropped a large piece of flesh and a loaf of Indian meal bread. They had evidently raided an open market. Quickly the old man had the provisions in the kettle on the fire. Mrs. Taylor continues:

"While the pot was still boiling, the door opened, and to his great delight his cousin, the priest, walked in.

" 'Look and see,' said the old man, smiling, as he indicated the simmering vessel on the fire.

"For some time the priest would not lift the lid, feeling sure there was nothing boiling there but water; but at length the savory odor was unmistakable, and overcome by curiosity, he peeped into the earthen pot. What was his astonishment when the dinner was revealed!

" 'Why,' he cried, 'where did you get this?'

"My heavenly Father sent it,' responded the old man, gladly. 'He put it into your heart, you know, to bring me a little millet from time to time; but when you would do so no longer, it was quite easy for Him to find another messenger.' And the whole incident, his prayer, and the coming of the ravens, was graphically told.

"The priest was so much impressed by what he saw and heard that he became from that time an earnest inquirer, and before long confessed his faith in Christ by baptism. He gave up his comfortable living in the temple for the blessed reality that now satisfied his soul. He supported himself as a teacher, became a much-respected deacon in the church, and during the Boxer troubles of 1900 endured terrible tortures, and finally laid down his life for Jesus' sake."

In Early Reformation Days

Cast into prison for the faith in Bohemia, Matthias Dolanscious was left by his persecutors without care. The history records:

"One day, when he was on the point of starving, he cast his eyes toward the grate of his prison window, and saw a little bird, perhaps a carrier pigeon, sitting there with something in his bill. His curiosity led him thither. The bird flew away, but left a bit of cloth, in which, when he took it up, he found a piece of gold; with this he found means to furnish himself with bread until he obtained full deliverance."

Reformer Brenz's Experience

Duke Ulric, of Stuttgart, had protected Johannes Brenz, of Würtemberg, one of the Reformed teachers in the sixteenth century. But the emperor had learned of the teacher's presence in the city, and sent a band of soldiers to take him. Brenz, forewarned, hastily sought God for guidance. We are told:

"He seemed to hear a voice saying: 'Take a loaf of bread, and go up through the Birkenwald [the upper part of the city was so called at that time]; and where you find an open front door, go in and hide yourself under the roof.'

"Brenz did so. All the doors in that part of the city were closed until he came to the Landhouse [later the Reformed church]. Here the door stood open. He entered without being seen by any one. Under the roof was a large pile of wood, behind which he hid himself.

"The next day the imperial officer, with his Spanish soldiers, arrived in Stuttgart. Soldiers were at once stationed at all city gates, even at the exit of the duke's palace. They searched every house in the city, and finally the soldiers came to the Landhouse. Brenz perceived the clang of arms, and heard their loud talking and cursing as they went from room to room. They also came to his hiding place under the roof, and thrust their spears through the woodpile behind which Brenz lay. But they did not find him, and two weeks later they left Stuttgart.

" 'Now they are gone, and, praise the Lord, they have not found him,'—thus Brenz heard the people talk on the street below.

"But how was Brenz able to sustain his life during that long time? On the first day of his concealment, toward noon, about eleven o'clock, came a hen and laid an egg behind the woodpile. This she did every day till the end of his stay there. This egg served to quench his thirst, while the loaf of bread satisfied his hunger. The hen ceased coming on the day on which the soldiers departed."

In the St. Bartholomew's Massacre

In Scott's "Life of Theo Agrippa d'Aubigné" is an account of the deliverance of Merlin, a Protestant pastor, in the days of the Huguenot Massacre, beginning on St. Bartholomew's Day, 1572.

When the massacre began in Paris, the famed old Admiral Coligny, leader of the Huguenots, knew that he was marked for death. "Save yourselves, my friends," he cried to his associates. "All is over with me. I have long prepared for death." Of Merlin, history says:

"Merlin, the admiral's minister, flying with Teligny, the admiral's son-in-law, on the approach of the murderers, in passing over the tops of the houses, fell into a hayloft, and was concealed by the hay that fell upon him. He lay there three days and a half, and was preserved from being famished by a hen which had her nest close by the place where he was concealed, and came daily to lay an egg."

Baird's history of the Huguenots notes that several of the Protestant pastors in those times "had wonderful escapes."

Succor on the Battlefield

During the World War, in early 1917, at a general meeting in Pforzheim, southern Germany, I met a man who was attending an institute for colporteurs, getting ready to go out with the gospel books. Because of wounds on the battlefield, he was released from military service. He told me how he had found the Lord. Before the war he had heard our Adventist preachers, but being irreligious, had given no heed to the teaching. In the war he was stricken down by shrapnel, wounded to the verge of death. The receding line of battle left him lying unconscious on the field. He awoke, alone, not able to rise, with the sound of humming bullets in the air above him. He told me:

"Next morning I was faint from loss of blood and hunger. I had a little food in my knapsack, but was too weak to turn over or to unbuckle my straps to get it. There I lay in my blood, helpless and giving myself up to die.

"Just then a hen came out from a farmhouse and laid an egg next to me. I reached out my hand and took it and ate it.

"Next morning the hen came again, and laid another egg by me. I took it.

"Next morning again it came; and the next, and the next —five days, and every morning an egg that just kept life in my body.

"Then the storm of battle had passed, and the sanitary corps were out on the field to search for any living. I saw them, and had just life enough to cry out, to let them know that I was alive.

"I was taken to the hospital, and began to recover. As I found my life was evidently spared, I thought of my remarkable deliverance. I felt that surely God had been merciful to me a sinner. I began to thank Him, and gave Him my heart. And when I was sent to my home, I hunted up the people whose lectures I had attended, and gave myself to the study of the Bible. Now I am rejoicing in the 'blessed hope.'"

A Message of Care From the Sea

When the temple tax was due in Jerusalem, Jesus sent a disciple to the sea to draw out a fish that carried the necessary piece of money in its mouth. An answer from the sea came to a poor man on the Baltic Sea—and a lesson to two of our colporteurs. A. Tonisson, leader in the book work in that region, passes on the report that two of his associates wrote to him:

"We saw in a very beautiful valley an old broken-down house in which lived a very poor family. The reason they were poor was because of much sickness in their home, and they therefore were in great need. We spoke to this family and gave them literature. The woman then said, 'God sent you to us.' As we were about to leave the place, we promised to come again in the evening to speak with them about the gospel message for this time.

"As we returned in the evening and entered the house, the man pointed to a large fish on the table, and explained to us that soon after we had left, he had gone to the seashore and prayed, 'O God, if these people who are coming to visit us are Thy people, permit me to secure food for them, for Thou knowest that I have nothing in my house to eat but a little bread. O Lord, Thou didst feed the five thousand people with five barley loaves and two small fish. I will have two people with me tonight, and, O Lord, do help me that I may be able to feed them.' He further said: 'I went to the sea and as I looked down toward the water, behold, there was a large fish. The water was not deep, and I hurried out to it and caught it without much effort. I brought the fish to the house, and my wife and I praised the Lord for His wonderful help in providing food. The fish weighed ten pounds, and no one in this neighborhood has ever seen such a large fish in this community.'

"We spent the evening with these people, explaining to them the truth, and we praise the Lord for this wonderful experience, for it has given us great courage to go forward in the work for Him."

So the apostle Paul cried out in the prison at Philippi, as he saw the warden about to take his life, thinking his prisoners had escaped during the earthquake that shook the walls and opened the prison doors. He knew the stern Roman penalty. And then Paul and Silas preached the gospel to the repentant man, who, with his family, was baptized.

In Postwar Europe

In the midst of the widespread unbelief and hopelessness of postwar Europe, our colporteurs renewed their efforts to carry the pages of light and hope to the people. One of our leaders in Europe, L. H. Christian, related this experience:

"In one of the Catholic countries a colporteur ringing a doorbell had no response. He rang again. He was about to turn away when the impression came to him that he should not cease his efforts. He rang again and again. Finally the door was opened by a man who expressed surprise. The man invited the colporteur in and listened to his canvass and talked with him, and his heart was touched. He then led the colporteur into a room where a rope was hanging from the rafters over a chair. The man said, 'When you came, I was on that chair with that rope around my neck, ready to take my life. Ten or twelve of us had agreed to commit suicide. I was to be the first. But when you rang and then continued to ring the second and the third time, something seemed to say, "Go and open the door. If you will go to the door, you will find something that will keep you from doing what you are about to do. God will help you." '

"The colporteur talked with the man about the way of life, prayed with him, and sold him a book. The man gave our colporteur the names and addresses of the others who had agreed to follow him, by death, out of the troubles of this world. Most of them bought books, and an interest sprang up. The man himself accepted the message, and as the result we have a good church in that place.

"Knock Again!"

To a colporteur waiting with no response at a door in Tasmania, came the impression, "Knock again!" The colporteur's story was told me by Evangelist L. D. A. Lemke, of Australia:

"He was a godly Christian man, and his brief visits were a blessing to many as he went from house to house taking orders. In one home in Tasmania he knocked and waited a moment with no response. He knocked again and again. No one answering, he was about to turn from the door when the impression came strongly upon him to remain and continue knocking. He knocked yet more earnestly for admittance, and in a few moments a woman appeared at the door. She looked disturbed.

" 'What do you want?' she asked.

" 'I am showing books that help the people to come closer to the Lord,' answered the colporteur.

"She invited him in. He described his book and talked with her of the Lord and His mercy and love. He then asked the privilege of praying, and engaged in earnest prayer. The woman invited him to come again. On his second visit, she said to him:

" 'Do you know what I was doing when you knocked at that door the first time you called?'

" 'No,' said the colporteur.

" 'Well,' she said, 'I was fixing a rope to take my life.'

"Today this woman is a rejoicing Seventh-day Adventist, a candidate for immortal life."

"Stop! Go to That House"

From South America comes the report of the experience of a woman colporteur, out among the people with the books that win souls:

"She was walking to her home one evening after her day's work. As she was passing a certain house, a voice said to her: 'Stop! Go to that house.' The voice was so clear and definite that the sister felt she must obey. She knocked repeatedly before there was any response. Finally a woman, with tears streaming down her cheeks, came. At first she would not let the colporteur in, but as the caller spoke of the love of Jesus, she admitted her. After prayer the woman told the colporteur that she had written a note to leave behind for her loved ones, and that when the knock came she was ready to take poison to end her life. 'Now,' she exclaimed, 'God has sent His angel to save me.' The colporteur took this woman to the meetings, and she became a Seventh-day Adventist. Her husband also accepted the truth and became a colporteur."

Turned Back to Life and Service

At an Autumn Council of the Seventh-day Adventist General Conference Committee, W. H. Branson, vice-president for the North American Division, related various special providences of the year in the evangelistic field, among these being the following:

"In San Francisco a woman in hopeless despair had boarded a streetcar on her way to the ferry to jump overboard in the Bay and drown herself. She passed our tabernacle, where Evangelist Boothby was holding public meetings. She saw there the advertisement of the meetings. She said to herself, 'I am going to hear one more sermon before I die.' She got off the streetcar and went into the meeting, to hear her funeral sermon, as she supposed. Her interest was awakened in the truth, and in life again; and today she rejoices in the message and in the blessing of living for the purpose of trying to bless others."

In Southern Europe

The leader of our colporteur work in Southern Europe, F. Charpiot, came in from one trip over his field with two reports of lifesaving calls by colporteurs. One was in German Switzerland:

"A woman at the door wept as the colporteur kindly inquired concerning the evident gloom and despair that was on her countenance. 'I have nothing to live for. My husband is a drunkard, and I suffer abuse and beatings. When you knocked,' she added, 'I was writing a farewell note to my children, and then was to end my life."

The Christian colporteur told of the hope in Christ, and prayed with her. Her heart was comforted, and her outlook changed.

In Jugoslavia another colporteur had found an elderly woman in tears, as he insistently knocked at the door:

" 'Why this grief, may I ask?' he said. The mother called her daughter, who came in with the picture of despair on her face. Then, after some time in conversation about God and His love for all, the visitor was taken into the barn in the rear. They showed there some cord, a bottle of poison, and a pistol. 'We were deciding which it was to be,' they said. Today these two are preparing for baptism and for a life of service with the children of God."

At the Right Moment

The late Morris Lukens, evangelist and executive, related the following account of the arrival of a woman magazine worker, in America, at the right door at the right moment:

"Our worker knocked twice at the door. No response. She was impressed to try again. A lady opened the door, saying, 'Come in.' She explained that she had been so depressed and hopeless over her situation that she had that morning decided to end her life. But as she was taking her last breakfast, as she thought, the impression came to her to pray. For the last few minutes she had been upstairs praying God to send some one to help her.

"Our worker well knew that she had been sent of God to answer that prayer. Earnestly she worked for that woman's soul. They became friends; and in time the woman was baptized into Christ and faith and hope."

THE TITHE AND PROVIDENCE

"Bring ye all the tithes into the storehouse, . . . and prove Me." Mal. 3:10.

In these promises through Malachi the Lord shows that faithfulness in tithes and offerings will enable Him to open the windows of heaven and "pour" out abundant blessings. Thousands have proved it. They tell of blessings poured out. It is primarily spiritual blessings; for the Lord is not promising wealth, riches of earth, to those who faithfully bring in the tithes and offerings for this cause. It is still "the poor of this world" who are "rich in faith."

A Sign to the World of Special Providence

Yet no one has ever been impoverished by faithfulness in giving to God the tenth of the income which is His. The world has really marveled at the amount Seventh-day Adventists have given, these many years, to missions. The figures of this church have been used far and wide by other churches, and in many lands, to encourage people to give for home work and missions "as the Seventh-day Adventists do." One Catholic editor said: "One Seventh-day Adventist gives as much as 200 Catholics." When, in days of decreased mission giving, during the early years of the depression, some great missionary societies were having to retreat and give up their mission stations, one leader who saw our work holding on said to our workers in a foreign field:

"That is to be expected of your work; for with the wonderful financial system you have [in the tithe], backed up by the loyalty of your people as no other organization is, we would expect you to be carrying on when all the rest of us have ceased to function."

Such publicity in many lands fulfills the promise in Malachi, where the Lord said to His people that if they would be faithful in tithes and offerings, "all nations shall call you blessed." Mal. 3:12. And the foreign mission gifts of Seventh-day Adventists are over and beyond the tithe. That of itself shows how the Lord does pour out temporal, material blessings for tithe-paying faithfulness. The gifts for missions beyond the tithe are a marvel to the world. Only the direct blessing of a providential Helper can account for it. The Lord said, "Prove Me now herewith," and in all parts of the earth men and women are continually telling how they have proved Him true. This is a continual world-wide token of the hand of Providence over a tithe-paying people's toil for a livelihood. It is a greater sign to the world than any individual experience can be. Yet individual experiences of providential care in this matter abound everywhere.

A Shoemaker's Test

In England, years ago, G. H. —— told how he was tested and how Providence wrought for him. He had a small shoeshop. Attending some evangelistic meetings, he heard the preaching of the Sabbath truth. "Well," he said to his wife, "I have barely made a living working all the week. Now if we must keep the Sabbath, I don't know how we shall come out. But it is right, and I will do it."

A little later, in the same meetings, he heard of the tithe. "Now, here I see my finish, wife," he said. "We have barely made it when I kept all I made. Now a tenth of what I make belongs to God. It is true, and we will do it. But how ever we are to get on I don't know."

I heard him tell it, many years ago. Only recently, reviewing the experience of those days, the brother told again how he did get on. The tithe was not his "finish." I quote his recently told story of the sequel:

"I had had a strong fight to accept the Sabbath, and a stronger fight to accept the doctrines of systematic tithe paying, and now I found myself in great prominence before the people of my town, and surrounding towns and villages.

"I was driven to pray as never before, but, thank God,

He gave me the victory. How He did so was an experience I shall never forget as long as I live.

"Just at this opportune time a firm in London wrote, asking if I made a certain boot. I inquired concerning this firm, and found that it was the largest in London. I felt that I never dared cater to such a firm as this, and I said, 'No;' but a few days later I was so impressed that I ought to try, that I sent a sample pair.

"In about four days I received an order that almost stunned me, for my business was carried on in a very small way.

"The order was for five thousand pairs. You may imagine how I felt. I said, 'I must have been foolish indeed to have led them on by sending that sample.' I did not know what to do. I knew my little shed would be absolutely no use for such an order as this. I could not get the leather in, much less make the shoes there. My house and shed combined would not hold the leather."

Suffice it to say, he got enlarged quarters, hired workmen, and carried on a manufacturing business employing many. Again and again he used to say, when the doctrine of the tithe was up for consideration in conference meetings, "I tell you, brethren, I know it is a good thing for a poor man to pay the tithe!"

Rebuking "the Devourer"

In the promise concerning faithfulness in tithe paying, the Lord says, "I will rebuke the devourer." Most of us can never know, till we learn in heaven, how often providential care has turned away the destroyer in our daily toil. We have been kept, and have found blessedness in making the Lord a real partner in our finances by that blessed tenth interest of His in our business. We have not paid the tithe into His storehouse—the temple treasury of old, the church treasury now —with any thought of financial returns. It is not temporal profit here on earth, but the eternal inheritance that we live for. As the world waxes old "like a garment," and the elements go awry, and the very things of nature decay, we may expect to suffer material loss with a suffering world. As the prophet speaks of these last-day conditions, he voices our faith:

"Although the fig tree shall not blossom, neither shall fruit be in the vines; the labor of the olive shall fail, and the fields shall yield no meat; the flock shall be cut off from the fold, and there shall be no herd in the stalls; yet I will rejoice in the Lord, I will joy in the God of my salvation." Hab. 3:17, 18.

However, in the midst of these destroying visitations, believers have often seen a Hand lifted up against the destroyer, as though to witness to the world that God can still deliver. Here again we may not be able to understand all these providences—why one must lose his goods in some visitation of trouble, while conspicuous deliverance comes at another time. We do not know why the disciple James was allowed to suffer martyrdom at Herod's hands, while an angel delivered Peter out of Herod's prison. We know James was as dear to God as Peter; and no doubt the death of James bore testimony to the sustaining grace of Christ with a power equal to any witness that Peter ever bore. The man whose faith enables him to rejoice in the Lord when the fig tree does not blossom and when the field yields no meat, is needed as a witness to the world as much as the one who can tell of special deliverance from "the devourer."

Caterpillars Turned Back

When on a visit to Australia, in 1918, I met several brethren who spoke of a deliverance that had come to the field of one new member in the time of a plague of caterpillars. Evangelist T. A. Brown, who was an eyewitness, related the story as follows:

"The district was visited by a plague of caterpillars, which destroyed acres of beautiful grain and grass crops. It seemed as if nothing could stop them. One man was the proud possessor of a particularly fine field of grass, soon to be cut for hay. The devastating pests bared his land as if it had been plowed and harrowed. Right beside it was an immense field of oats belonging to one of the brethren lately come into the truth. This brother watched the caterpillars, like Attila's hordes, pouring through the fence toward his crop. His workman, who is not a Seventh-day Adventist, standing by, remarked quite seriously, 'You need not fear; they will not touch your oats, because you keep the commandments of God.' And so it was. Our heavenly Father was true to His promise in Malachi 3 :11.

"On visiting there some days afterward, I saw the dead bodies of these devourers lying thick along the edge of the oats, as if the angel of God had allowed them to come to the danger point, then 'breathed in the face of the foe as he passed,' smiting them with death before they touched one blade. The bare acres on one side of the wire fence, and the full waving heads of strong, healthy oats on the other, were an overwhelming evidence of the reality of God and of His fidelity to His promises."

As I talked of the experience with those who had seen the deliverance, our farmer brother, whose heart was very tender at the thought of it, told me how he stood by his fence watching. "I got down by the fence alone," he said, "and prayed the Lord to help me." He was new in this way and in religious experience, having but just begun to yield obedience to the Lord's truth. He knew the Lord had delivered him, he said. But because of his indebtedness in getting started, he had not as yet begun to pay the Lord's tithe. So it went on until the next year's crops were well grown. Then again the insect grubs appeared in the fields. He got a neighbor, one of our brethren, to go quickly down to get poison with which to fight the grubs and to save as much of his crop as possible.

"I determined then and there," he said, "that henceforth I would give to the Lord the tithe, whatever came."

He felt that God had blessed him the year before in a marvelous way, rebuking the devourer, and that he had not kept faith with God. A new and deeper experience came to him as he faced what seemed inevitable disaster. The neighbor came with the poison, and went out into the fields to begin the fight. Soon, however, he came back to the house, saying:

"You don't need to put the poison out. The caterpillars are climbing down the stalks and leaving the field."

And so it actually was. I saw brethren at the general meeting who testified that of a truth the caterpillars forsook the place, leaving the waving field as a testimony to the delivering hand of God.

Pleading the Promise of Malachi 3:11

Here is another story of the deliverance of one of our Australian farmer brethren, Mr. P——. I heard it at a camp meeting there in 1930. After two or three bad seasons on a rented farm, his current season's wheat crop promised to save him from financial embarrassment. Then, suddenly, the locusts came. The invaders had swept fields next to him so clean that the ground was bare. Now they were on the edge of his field.

What to do he knew not. Some said, "Run a roller over them." "I tried that," the brother told me, "but the roller had no appreciable effect on the crawling army." That night it seemed certain that another season's crop was lost. It meant sore financial trouble. Our brother took it to God in prayer.

He himself did not tell me the details. He felt unworthy to receive special blessings. Yet he knew God had intervened. But Evangelist C. J. Reynolds, of northern New South Wales, who was there, told me the story. He says our brother talked the matter over with his wife. "Wife," he said, "is there anything wrong in my life, in the way I am living—any change that I must make in order to claim the promises of God?"

"I don't know of anything, husband," the wife replied.

Then, at the family altar of prayer that doleful night, they laid their situation before God, pleading the promise of Malachi 3:11. Next morning early our brother came for Mr. Reynolds. "Come, quickly,'" he called. "It sounded like a call to come and see the desolation wrought. I expected to find nothing but ruin," said our evangelist; "but what I saw was dead locusts lying so thick over the ground that their bodies filled all the little hollows and depressions in the ground. They had begun on the two corners of Brother P——'s field, but they were suddenly smitten with death. The wheat field was there intact, save for a small portion at the two corners, where the locusts had begun, when death smote them."

I was told that one farm workman, who had not been a Christian, was converted. He knew that he had seen the workings of the divine Hand, and that God had wrought for one who trusted Him.

Again Devourers Smitten

It was in Western Canada that A. V. Rhoads, president of a conference, visited the home of Mr. and Mrs. C-——. He says:

"While we were at the table, enjoying the bounties which nature had provided for us, the good hostess told us that the Lord had given them this food by a special miracle. She stated that insects in large armies were eating the neighbors' gardens and were coming over the line into her garden. She took her Bible and read the promise in Malachi: 'I will rebuke the devourer for your sakes.' She and her husband knelt in prayer, knowing that they had been faithful in tithe paying. Arising from their knees, they went out into the garden. They saw that the insects had already begun work on it, but on examination they found the insects had been smitten with death, and many were lying dead under the vines, having done very little damage."

Praying in the Midst of the Field

In the southern part of the island of Negros, in the Philippines, a plague of locusts came down upon the sugar-cane fields. Evangelist R. B. Cahilig reported how a woman of our church there met the crisis. Her husband is not a member, but all along has allowed his wife to tithe all income.

"While the others were beating their empty petroleum cans for the purpose of scaring the locusts away, our sister went into the midst of her sugar-cane field and knelt there, praying God to save her plantation and to fulfill His promise to her that very hour. After that she went home trusting all to His care.

"The next morning this sister went out to see her sugar-cane plantation, and found that not a single stalk was destroyed. But those of her neighbors had been entirely eaten during the night. The people wondered at such a mystery. Some told her that she was *antinganting* (a charm of magic), and others said that maybe she placed a *paningalap* (safeguard of protection supposed to be supernatural) in the midst of her farm. Then our sister began to tell them that it was because she was faithful in paying her tithes to the Lord. 'That was the cause,' she told them, 'God took care of my sugar-cane plantation. He rebuked the devourer for my sake,' she finished."

"Windows of Heaven Opened"

That is how Superintendent V. T. Armstrong, of the Japan Union Mission, described the experience of a Japanese believer:

"In one of the country districts of Japan is a little country church of faithful, God-fearing farmers. They love the message. The elder of the church believes in his members' holding high the principles of truth.

"One spring during rice-planting time a real test came to him. The rice plants had been delivered on Thursday ready for planting on Friday. But because of a storm it was impossible for the plants to be set out. Sabbath morning was bright and clear, and on all sides neighbors were busily setting out plants; but this brother, along with the other members of the church, was faithful to the command of God. His neighbors laughed at him and told him his plants would be ruined and his crop a failure. Then they laughed at his religion and his God. But our brother prayed God to fulfill His promise.

He was a commandment keeper, both in keeping the Sabbath and in paying a faithful tithe. Although his plants did look a little wilted, in a few days they were growing well, and before long were ahead of the plants in the neighboring fields. By harvesttime our faithful member had the largest rice crop in the neighborhood. It was an astonishment to all.

"At harvesttime God especially protected this brother's crop. A great storm came beating the fields of grain into the ground; but our brother had been impressed to work the whole Saturday night before, taking in his grain; and when the storm came, his crop was safe. The neighbors all said his God had blessed him."

A Witness to the Neighbors

From Argentina, South America, J. H. Meier sent to the *Review and Herald* an account of a believer's deliverance from all-devouring locusts. He lived far remote from others of like faith, but always sent in his tithe. One day the sky was darkened, and clouds of locusts settled on the land all about our brother's place.

"They ate up everything,—wheat, corn, fruit, even the bark off the trees. They came up to our brother's land, but to the astonishment of the neighbors they did not enter his field, where he had a good prospect for a fine crop of wheat. His crop was untouched, while all around his farm everything was eaten, not a leaf or blade remaining.

"The neighbors began to talk about it, and said he must be *santo,* or holy. They asked him why it was that the Lord protected him and not the rest of them. He told them that he believed the Bible, and that it taught that we should keep the Sabbath and pay tithes and offerings; that this was what he did, and therefore the Lord protected him. He read to them Malachi 3:7-11. They were astonished.

"The incident attracted so much attention that even the judge of the city went out to see the protected wheat, and our brother had an opportunity to read this text to him."

Deliverance, Disaster, and Deliverance

As a lesson for all time, evidently, Providence allowed Satan, the destroyer, "the prince of the power of the air," to sweep away Job's possessions. But the apostle James admonishes us to look to "the end of the Lord" in that matter of Job's troubles. James 5:11. As we look to the end, we see Job's patience and trust in all the times of trouble, and his final deliverance. Here is a narrative set down years ago by Evangelist M. N. Campbell:

"G. K——, when still a farmer in Wisconsin and young in the faith, had his attention drawn to the tithing system. He was poor and lived on a rented farm. He decided that, in view of the promise of Malachi 3:10, he could well afford to adopt tithing. His crops that year were the best. He told in his testimony one Sabbath how the Lord had fulfilled His word in prospering his crops in return for his faithfulness in tithe paying. That afternoon a terrific windstorm blew his crops to the four winds, leaving him penniless.

"For a little while Mr. K—— was in deep despair over the apparent failure of God to live up to His promise. But his faithful wife suggested that God was not limited to that crop in the matter of bestowing His blessing. His waning faith returned, and he believed the promise in the face of calamity, and God opened the windows of heaven and blessed him with a surprising degree of temporal prosperity. He soon became owner of the farm he was renting. He was later called to the gospel ministry, and always bore a strong testimony in favor of tithe paying."

Keeping Exact Accounts With God

At a district convention for the West Visayan section of the Philippine group, Missionary W. H. Bergherm heard a member relate this story of keeping the accounts exact with God:

"When the truth found me, I was working in a sugar central (refinery) in Negros for 100 pesos a month. I knew that if I should be baptized, I would undoubtedly lose my job.

My relatives, who were depending upon me for their support, were determined that I should never be baptized. After baptism, I was discharged from the central. With a very small capital I opened up a little *tienda* (shop). But our business did not prosper. Our relatives persecuted us, trying to drive me back to my work at the central, and so cause me to transgress the law of God. During this time we were not careful in the paying of an honest tithe. Our business continued to lose and our children were often sick.

"One day my wife and I sat down and talked it over. We could not go on as we had, and then and there we decided to try God out to the full. We began to make a careful record of all our business and to pay a full tithe. The change was wonderful. Our business began to prosper at once. In spite of hard times, we always have plenty of customers, and our living is easier and better than it was when we were supported by the central."

The Way Out of Debt

When leading a conference in the southwestern part of the United States, the following experience came to the attention of J. F. Wright, now president of the Southern African Division:

"A farmer died and left a farm to his sons. There were debts amounting to $6,000. The sons, who were Adventists, felt they could not give any of the proceeds of the farm to God until the debts were all paid. They cultivated the farm on that basis for three years, with little headway in getting out of debt. Then, from a study of the word of God, they agreed that they would give at least a tenth of the net proceeds to the Lord for His work. Through the next year they paid the tithe on all the increase. And in that fourth year they cleared off more of the debts on the farm than they had in the other three years put together. 'Them that honor Me, I will honor.'"

"I Paid My Tithe and—!"

In a pamphlet under the above title Editor A. S. Maxwell, of the British journal, *Present Truth,* gathered many incidents of tithing providences. Here are two testimonies illustrative of experiences in the common workaday world of toil and struggle:

The Pound Note.—A brother, tempted in the time of acute need to borrow from his tithe, was counseled against it by his wife. And in telling of it, he says:

"Suddenly I noticed my Bible on the table, and said, 'Well, let us see what the Scripture says on this matter.' So I opened it, and in Jonah 2:9 read these words: 'I will pay that that I have vowed. Salvation is of the Lord.'

"Convinced that God was speaking to me through His word, I placed the money in an envelope, and took it round to the one who was responsible for collecting the tithe. That night my family retired to bed hungry.

"In the morning the postman delivered a letter which, when opened, was found to contain a note for £1, and a slip of paper bearing these words: 'The Lord has impressed me that you are in need. Please accept the enclosed from a friend.'

"No signature, no address—simply our heavenly Father supplying our needs after we had proved Him, as advised in Malachi 3:10, 11. To this day we do not know the name of our benefactor.

"But God's blessing did not stop there. As a result of this experience I have consistently and faithfully paid tithe, and as a direct result have been blessed financially above my highest expectations as a colporteur-evangelist. Looking back on past experiences, I can trace God's loving presence in my life from the day when I obeyed His word: 'Bring ye all the tithes into the storehouse, . . . and prove Me now herewith, saith the Lord of hosts.' "—*C. L. K.*

A House Sold.—"A few years ago I adopted the Bible system of tithing. For a time all went well. Then came a day when God permitted my source of income to be taken away, and the test came. I had a difficult situation to face without future prospects. My only possessions were fifty shillings tithe due, and a house that I had been unable to sell for over three years. The temptation came to withhold the tithe until circumstances were more favorable.

"Then there came to me the promise of God in Malachi 3:10. I stepped out in faith and paid the tithe, trusting Him who had promised.

"Within four hours the Lord sent the means to earn nearly three times the tithe, and within a month my house was sold.

"The Lord asks us to prove Him. I have done so and praise His name. He has never failed."—*L. M. H.*

A Mother's Prayer

In the Inter-American Division *Messenger*, W. R. Elliott, of the Caribbean Union Conference, told the following story of a mother's trust in time of need. Her husband had gone from home to take up work. He had left what money he had. But before he could send home anything from his pay, the mother's funds had given out. There was no food for the children's breakfast.

"The mother was perplexed. She had no money except one dollar, and it was the Lord's tithe. Must she take it and buy bread for her children? There seemed no other way out for her, and yet she felt that it would be wrong to spend the tithe in that way, and scarcely knew what to do. She took the dollar out of the trunk, called her children about her and told them it was tithe, and that they ought not to use it, not even to buy food. Then she and her little ones knelt down and told the Lord all about their distress and hunger, and asked Him to help them in their trouble. While on her knees she told the Lord she would not spend the dollar of tithe, and asked Him to help her. She arose from prayer, went to the trunk, and placed the money in the bottom of it, and relocked the trunk.

"In a few minutes some little thing called her to go out of the yard and down an old unused path a little way, and there in the path lay a bright silver dollar before her. She picked it up, gave thanks to God for so quickly, and in such an unusual way, giving her the answer to her prayer, and then went to a store some distance away and purchased food for herself and her children. That dollar lasted until the husband was able to send them money on which to live.

"I heard her relate this story of God's loving care one day in a testimony meeting at the church, and no one could convince her that God did not give her a direct answer to her prayer that day as she and her little ones knelt before Him and told Him of their hunger, and asked Him for help."

"The time would fail me," said the writer of the epistle to the Hebrews, as he recounted deliverances in the Old Testament days. So, assuredly, the time fails us now to record more of these stories of tithe paying. They abound in our reports—from North and South America, from Africa, Asia, Europe, Australia, and all the islands of the sea. The living God does care for temporal needs, and sustains and blesses in prosperity or in adversity.

www.ingramcontent.com/pod-product-compliance
Lightning Source LLC
Chambersburg PA
CBHW060545100426
42742CB00013B/2459